11/19/08

34.50

DATE			

The Progressive Era

Other titles in the American History series

AMERICAN HISTORY

The Progressive Era

Kevin Hillstrom

LUCENT BOOKS

A part of Gale, Cengage Learning

GALE
CENGAGE Learning

Detroit • New York • San Francisco • New Haven, Conn • Waterville, Maine • London

LIBRARY OF CONGRESS CATALOGING-IN-PUBLICATION DATA

Hillstrom, Kevin, 1963–
  The Progressive Era / by Kevin Hillstrom.
    p. cm. — (American history)
  Includes bibliographical references and index.
  ISBN 978-1-4205-0067-7 (hardcover)
  1. United States—History—1865–1921—Juvenile literature. 2. United States—Social conditions—1865–1918—Juvenile literature. 3. United States—Politics and government—Juvenile literature. 4. Progressivism (United States politics)—Juvenile literature. I. Title.
  E661.H56 2009
  324.2732'7—dc22

                                                                    2008025569

Lucent Books
27500 Drake Rd
Farmington Hills MI 48331

ISBN-13: 978-1-4205-0067-7
ISBN-10: 1-4205-0067-8

Printed in the United States of America
1 2 3 4 5 6 7 12 11 10 09 08

Contents

Foreword

The United States has existed as a nation for just over 200 years. By comparison, Rome existed as a nation-state for more than 1000 years. Out of a few struggling British colonies, the United States developed relatively quickly into a world power whose policy decisions and culture have great influence on the world stage. What events and aspirations drove this young American nation to such great heights in such a short period of time? The answer lies in a close study of its varied and unique history. As James Baldwin once remarked, "American history is longer, larger, more various, more beautiful, and more terrible than anything anyone has ever said about it."

The basic facts of United States history—names, dates, places, battles, treaties, speeches, and acts of Congress—fill countless textbooks. These facts, though essential to a thorough understanding of world events, are rarely compelling for students. More compelling are the stories in history, the experience of history.

Titles in this series explore the history of the country and the experiences of Americans. What influences led the colonists to risk everything and break from Britain? Who was the driving force behind the Constitution? Which factors led thousands of people to leave their homelands and settle in the United States? Questions like these do not have simple answers; by discussing them, however, we can view the past as a more real, interesting, and accessible place.

Students will find excellent tools for research and investigation in every title. Lucent Books' American History series provides not only facts, but also the analysis and context necessary for insightful critical thinking about history and about current events. Fully cited quotations from historical figures, eyewitnesses, letters, speeches, and writings bring vibrancy and authority to the text. Annotated bibliographies allow students to evaluate and locate sources for further investigation. Sidebars highlight important and interesting figures, events, or related primary source excerpts. Timelines, maps, and full color images add another dimension of accessibility to the stories being told.

It has been said the past has a history of repeating itself, for good and ill. In these pages, students will learn a bit about both and, perhaps, better understand their own place in this world.

Important Dates at the Time

1880
Vincent Van Gogh begins painting.

1896
The U.S. Supreme Court rules in *Plessy v. Ferguson* that "separate but equal" racial segregation is legal; this decision solidifies "Jim Crow" laws in the American South.

1858
The first transatlantic cable is laid between Britain and the United States.

1850	1855	1860	1865	1870	1880	1885	1890	1895

1889
Jane Addams founds Hull House, which becomes the model for Progressive Era social relief organizations.

1901
Theodore Roosevelt becomes president of the United States after the assassination of William McKinley.

1898
Spanish American War

1902
Cuba declares independence from the United States and Spain.

of the Progressive Era

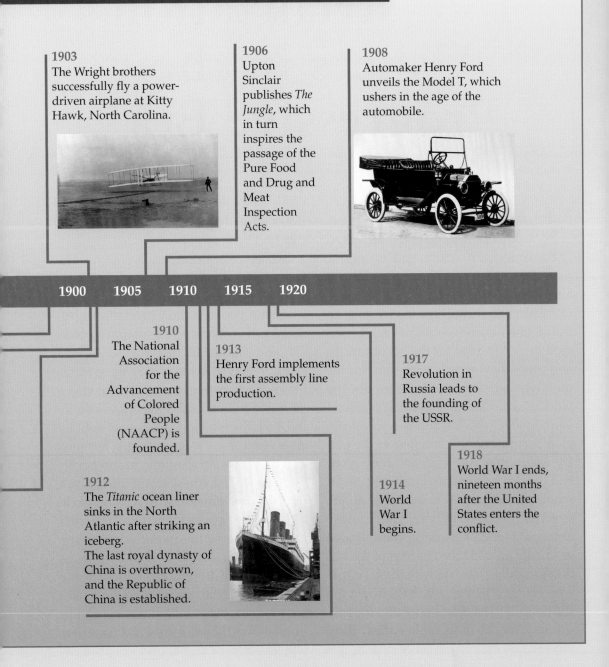

1903
The Wright brothers successfully fly a power-driven airplane at Kitty Hawk, North Carolina.

1906
Upton Sinclair publishes *The Jungle*, which in turn inspires the passage of the Pure Food and Drug and Meat Inspection Acts.

1908
Automaker Henry Ford unveils the Model T, which ushers in the age of the automobile.

1900   1905   1910   1915   1920

1910
The National Association for the Advancement of Colored People (NAACP) is founded.

1913
Henry Ford implements the first assembly line production.

1917
Revolution in Russia leads to the founding of the USSR.

1912
The *Titanic* ocean liner sinks in the North Atlantic after striking an iceberg.
The last royal dynasty of China is overthrown, and the Republic of China is established.

1914
World War I begins.

1918
World War I ends, nineteen months after the United States enters the conflict.

Introduction

Industrialization Ushers in the Progressive Era

The industrial revolution of the nineteenth century greatly increased American wealth and economic productivity, but these advances came at a tremendous cost. The factories, mills, railroads, and steamships that sprang up during the nation's industrial age generated huge fortunes for the corporations and trusts that owned them—and for the men who led those businesses. But the workers who toiled in the nation's railroad yards, mines, oil fields, and factories struggled to support their families on the paltry wages they received, and they often had to work under dangerous and dehumanizing conditions. This state of affairs sparked great resentment and anger among America's working class. It also gradually aroused the concern of the nation's middle class. Many of these people were shocked by the contrast between the suffering of the nation's poor and the luxurious lifestyles of its millionaires. They viewed this situation as proof that the na-

tion's lofty ideals of justice and opportunity had been forgotten.

Millions of working-class and middle-class Americans felt that they were powerless to stand against the railroad magnates, bankers, and manufacturing tycoons who controlled the nation's political and industrial machines. As the century drew to a close, "the United States was not one nation, but several; it was a land divided by region, race, and ethnicity. And it was a land still deeply split by class conflict . . . wage workers, farmers, and the rich were alien to one another."[1]

In response to these troubling times, a popular movement known as progressivism swept across the nation in the first two decades of the twentieth century. This movement was driven by groups with many different priorities. Some were dedicated to addressing the crushing poverty and terrible working conditions that afflicted industrial America. Others set their sights on fixing the nation's problems of political corruption and gender discrimination.

The leadership of the Progressive movement also was wide-ranging. It included individuals from President Theodore Roosevelt, woman suffrage advocate Alice Paul, and journalist Upton Sinclair to social reformer Jane Addams, anti-alcohol evangelist Billy Sunday, Socialist firebrand Eugene Debs, and labor leader Mary "Mother" Jones. But even though the causes and methods of these leaders and their organizations varied enormously, they shared a basic goal of reforming and improving American society for the benefit of all.

Finally, the activists and supporters of reform during America's Progressive Era shared a similar view of the American government and its appropriate role in the lives of its citizens. They believed that the economic and social forces unleashed by the industrial revolution required government to take a more active role in managing the nation's fortunes than it had ever done before. Unlike earlier generations of Americans who had been suspicious of government regulation of the marketplace, business operations, and civil rights, the leaders of the so-called Age of Reform argued that only the government had the power to curb the excesses of big business and

treat the social ills that threatened American communities. The Progressive movement declared that if the government did not step in, America itself was in danger of crashing down in a storm of violence and chaos.

These warnings were heeded. During the first two decades of the twentieth century, municipal, state, and federal governments became much more involved in addressing the nation's pressing economic and social problems. Numerous agencies and laws were created to fight poverty, pollution, exploitation of workers and

President Theodore Roosevelt, depicted in this political cartoon, was one of the leading advocates of the Progressive movement.

immigrants, and political corruption. Lawmakers also passed wide-reaching laws designed to address perceived social problems (such as the Eighteenth Amendment, which ushered in the age of Prohibition) and areas of social injustice (like the Nineteenth Amendment, which gave women the vote).

Many of the laws and regulatory powers assumed by the government during this era remain in force today, nearly a century after the Progressive Era came to an end. They govern the ways, both large and small, that Americans live, work, and do business. The continued importance of these laws and agencies to the fabric of American life provides compelling proof that the voices of the Progressive movement still echo in modern American society.

Chapter One

The Age of Industrialization

America's society and economy were forever changed by the fantastic mechanical inventions and business innovations that were introduced in the nineteenth century. Inventions such as the cotton gin, the steam engine, and the flying shuttle (a device that was instrumental in the creation of the textile industry) dramatically increased the efficiency of businesses. They greatly expanded economic activity in the cities and countryside alike. In this way, the United States followed the pattern of England, which had become the first industrialized nation back in the eighteenth century.

But while many of the people of England had greeted the industrial age with an attitude of skeptical suspicion, most Americans initially welcomed the industrial revolution with open arms. "There was widespread interest and approval in the United States for any device that could augment labor and diminish the human work requirement," explained one scholar. "Americans were used to having change bring betterment, and they reached for [steam power and other tools of industrialization] with curiosity and eagerness. For the workers, machines could lighten the drudgery of a great many tasks that had formerly called for muscle power. For consumers, machines brought more goods, usually at lower prices."[2]

America's embrace of new mass production manufacturing techniques, combined with its use of revolutionary new modes of transportation such as steamships and trains, brought enormous changes to the country's economy and culture in the early and mid-1800s. The huge impact of these changes was further heightened by two other simultaneous developments: the opening of the American West to settlement and the massive influx of European immigrants into the United States.

Immigrants and Industrial America

Railroads, the telegraph, and other creations of the industrial age greatly eased the opening and settlement of the West—which in turn encouraged further investment in factories, railroads, telegraph systems, logging, mining, ranching, and farming. But none of these developments could have taken place with such dizzying speed if it had not been for the tremendous influx of immigrants into America during the nineteenth century. These farmers, laborers, and merchants arrived by the millions with each passing decade. They provided the nation's factories, coal mines, stockyards, and steel foundries with the workers they needed to thrive. Immigrants also were a major force in the settlement of the Western wilderness. In short, they provided the young American nation with a massive infusion of muscle, sweat, ambition, and determination at a time when such assets were badly needed. Without their contributions, the industrialization and economic growth of America would have unfolded at a much slower pace.

The first great surge of immigrants who came to America in the nineteenth century fled poverty, starvation, and political repression in northern and western Europe. From 1815 to 1860, more than 5 million immigrants, mainly hailing from England, Ireland, Germany, and Scandinavia, made the arduous journey across

In the mid-1800s, millions of European immigrants, such as these Irish coal miners, helped prepare the United States for the industrial age.

the Atlantic Ocean to the United States. These new arrivals—along with immigrants from China and Mexico who moved into the Western territories—were instrumental in the settlement of the West. Irish coal miners, Swedish farmers, Chinese railroad workers, Norwegian loggers, and German meatpackers all played an important role in converting the resources of the West into fuel for the country's fast-growing economic engine.

After 1880 the ethnic makeup of new arrivals to America underwent a dramatic shift. The tide of immigration shifted to eastern and southern Europe, and by the close of the nineteenth century immigrants from these regions accounted for nearly half of all immigrants to America. Immigrants from Italy, Poland, Hungary, Russia, and other eastern and southern European countries accounted for an even greater percentage of new arrivals in the first years of the twentieth century. By 1900 more than 26 million people in America—more than one out of three people in the country—were either immigrants or native-born Americans with at least one foreign-born parent.[3] Many of these workers were unskilled. This means they were untrained in trades that required specialized skills or knowledge, and so they had little choice but to use their sweat and muscle in the factories of the nation's great cities or the farmlands of the Midwest and Great Plains.

Social Darwinism

During these same decades, an influential idea known as social Darwinism took root in the nation's boardrooms, newspaper offices, and statehouses. This idea was advanced by influential thinkers such as American sociologist William Graham Sumner and English philosopher Herbert Spencer. It was based on the research of scientist Charles Darwin, who in the mid-nineteenth century had developed the theory of natural evolution that is widely recognized today. Darwin asserted that animals evolved over time, and that those creatures that were best adapted to survive (because of greater strength, speed, intelligence, or other characteristics) passed their genetic traits on to future generations. Over time, stated Darwin, the passing of these superior characteristics from generation to generation created more highly evolved species.

Spencer, Sumner, and other advocates of social Darwinism used this "survival of the fittest" concept to explain the dramatic differences in economic class that were emerging in America and other industrializing nations. They asserted that the fittest members of society were naturally the ones who attained the greatest wealth. According to this argument, poor people simply did not have the intelligence, ambition, or willpower to succeed in the new world of industrial commerce.

The wealthy men who controlled America's railroads, factories, banks, and mills welcomed this theory, as did many middle-class Americans who had worked hard to carve out comfortable lives for themselves and their families. Social Darwinism not only allowed the wealthy to view themselves as the "best" citizens of the nation, it also gave them a scientific excuse to ignore the terrible poverty afflicting millions of Americans.

Social Darwinism also fit together with America's historical enthusiasm for individualism and self-sufficiency. All of the country's most important founding documents, from the Declaration of Independence to the Constitution, "proclaimed the dignity and worth of the individual," wrote one historian. "The relentless spread of capitalism reaffirmed the individualist creed, but with a new emphasis on each person's ownership of his or her labor."[4]

The Robber Barons

Some of America's most powerful men were not shy about expressing their belief in the importance of individuality in American capitalism. They also embraced the concept of social Darwinism. The famous industrialist Andrew Carnegie, for example, declared that "only through exceptional individuals [has humanity] been able to ascend. . . . [It] is the leaders who do the new things that count, all these have been Individualistic to a degree beyond ordinary men and worked in perfect freedom; each and every one a character unlike anybody else; an original; gifted beyond most others of his kind, hence his leadership." [5]

Many of the country's political leaders shared Carnegie's beliefs. They condemned critics—especially poor ones—who dared to suggest that the stark contrast between the lives of America's wealthy industrialists and those of its impoverished working class might actually stem from greed and social injustice. In his 1901 memoir, for example, former U.S. president Benjamin Harrison declared that "the indiscriminate denunciation of the rich is mischievous. It perverts the mind, poisons the heart and furnishes an excuse to crime. No poor man was ever made richer or happier by it."[6]

These beliefs contributed to the ever-more-ruthless nature of American business in the 1800s. Many of the railroad tycoons, land developers, and factory owners who built their fortunes during this era did so by double-crossing business associates, bribing officials, and squeezing every last bit of sweat out of underpaid and exhausted workers. Their behavior led ordinary Americans to refer to these powerful men as robber barons. Ignoring the pivotal role that these flawed but ambitious men played in building America into an economic superpower, critics condemned the robber barons as coldhearted monsters who made their riches by exploiting the poor and vulnerable.

The Gilded Age

This image of greed and selfishness became even more widespread during America's so-called Gilded Age, which unfolded during the last two decades of the nineteenth century. During these years the nation's wealthiest men and women showed off their fortunes in ways that the country had never seen before. At a time when the average American household brought in less than twelve hundred dollars annually—and countless children went to bed hungry

Steel Magnate Andrew Carnegie

Andrew Carnegie (1835–1919) was one of the most famous businessmen in U.S. history. Born in Scotland in November 1835, he immigrated with his family to America in 1848. Carnegie first made his mark in railroads before jumping into the steel business after the Civil War. Investing heavily in steel mills that harnessed the latest technology, Carnegie became one of the most powerful figures in the steel industry by the late 1870s.

Over the last two decades of the nineteenth century, Carnegie also diversified into many other industries, including coal and iron mining and railroads. Carnegie used these properties to make his steel business even more profitable. In 1901 Carnegie sold his interest in the Carnegie Steel Company for more than $400 million. This epic business deal, which was brokered by J.P. Morgan, was part of a merger of eight steel companies that created U.S. Steel.

Carnegie lived in luxury for the rest of his life, but he also gave away large sums of money to various foundations and charitable causes. By the time of Carnegie's death, his reputation as a ruthless businessman and exploiter of workers had been at least partially erased by his years of generous donations to the arts and sciences.

Source: David Nasaw, *Andrew Carnegie.* New York: Penguin, 2006.

every night—"the rich [spent] tens of thousands of dollars on dinner parties where guests dined off solid-gold plates or, as at one given by Caroline Astor, [used] sterling-silver trowels to dig through heaps of sand arranged on the table to find buried treasure troves of diamonds and rubies."[7]

The most notorious symbols of America's Gilded Age were a few dozen families that rode the wave of industrialization to truly stunning levels of wealth and comfort. These fortunes were built by some of the most famous businessmen in U.S. history—men such as Carnegie, real estate mogul John Ja-cob Astor III, financier J.P. Morgan, oil tycoon John D. Rockefeller, and railroad magnates Cornelius Vanderbilt, Jay Gould, and Edward H. Harriman. These men used their wealth to acquire huge mansions, sprawling estates, sleek yachts, private railway cars, and stables of racehorses.[8]

Their fortunes were passed on to sons and daughters who swaddled themselves in extravagant luxury. All four of Vanderbilt's grandsons, for example, lived on great estates on the banks of New York State's Hudson River. All of these homes were virtual palaces, but the one built by the youngest grandson,

During the so-called Gilded Age, America's wealthiest families—Carnegie, Morgan, Rockefeller, and others—stood in stark contrast to the majority of Americans who were poor or struggling middle class.

George, rivaled the greatest castles of Europe. His Biltmore Estate, as it was known, was completed in 1895 in the heart of North Carolina's Blue Ridge Mountains. The 250-room mansion was the centerpiece of a 146,000-acre estate (59,084ha) that included its own reservoirs, schools, dairy farms, and hospital. After George Vanderbilt took up residence there, the Biltmore employed more workers than the entire U.S. Department of Agriculture.[9]

Rumblings of Rebellion

American newspapers and magazines provided extensive coverage of the lifestyles of America's rich and famous. These periodicals were the primary sources of news and information for Americans in this era, before the development of radio, television, and the Internet. The published accounts of fancy costume balls, lavish dinner parties, and casual shopping sprees for expensive jewelry and art were received with mounting anger and disapproval by much of the rest of the country.

Some of this anger stemmed from feelings of envy. But many Americans were disgusted by such displays of wealth at a time when poverty and hopelessness dominated so many tenement slums and factory floors. Most working-class men and women at the turn of the century believed that the nation's wealthy elite were using their economic and political power to keep their fellow citizens in subordinate economic positions. They felt that the rules handed down by corporate bosses and their political allies gave them little opportunity to improve their place in American society. As union leader John Mitchell stated, "[The American laborer] understands that working men do not evolve into capitalists as boys evolve into men or as caterpillars evolve into butterflies."[10]

Grangers Join Forces

The first significant reform movement of the post–Civil War era was the Grange Movement. The Grange was a farmers' organization that had originally been founded in the late 1860s to provide educational and social services to isolated farming families. In the 1870s, though, local Grange organizations in the upper Midwest and the South became politically energized by the ruthless business practices of American railroads, banks, and grain elevator companies. They complained that steep rail freight rates, soaring interest rates on bank loans, and inflated storage fees from grain elevators threatened to drive hardworking farmers out of business.

Frustrated and angry, the Grangers put political pressure on state legislatures to address these problems. As a result, a flurry of so-called "Granger laws" were passed. These laws placed restrictions on the rates that railroads and grain elevators could charge their customers. These laws were challenged by the corporations in court without success. By the mid-1870s the national Grange membership had reached 800,000 members. The influence of the Grange movement rapidly declined after that, though, because of poor leadership, disorganization, and petty jealousies.

Many of the problems that had sparked the birth of the Grange movement still remained, however. In the 1880s a movement to fight back against big business and political corruption arose out of America's heartland. The Populist movement developed in the agricultural communities of the South, Great Plains, and Midwest.

Populists Take Up the Call for Change

Populists believed that the federal government had a moral and legal duty to limit corporate power and address other problems of the industrial age. They called for federal ownership of the nation's railroad, telegraph, and telephone industries in order to ensure fair prices for all citizens. They also lobbied for changes to the American monetary system that would benefit farmers and working-class people. Another Populist priority was the establishment of a graduated personal income tax system—one in which poor Americans would pay a lower percentage of their income in taxes than rich Americans. In addition, the Populists wanted to restrict foreign immigration into the United States because they viewed immigrants as a threat to the jobs and wages of native-born Americans.

The 1892 Populist Party Platform

In 1892 the Populist Party chose Iowa politician James Weaver as its candidate in that year's presidential election. He ultimately attracted more than 8 percent of the popular vote to finish third behind Republican incumbent Benjamin Harrison (43 percent) and Democrat Grover Cleveland (46 percent), who won the election. Weaver ran on a platform that reflected the Populist movement's hostility to big business and industrialism. Below are excerpts from the platform's preamble:

We meet in the midst of a nation brought to the verge of moral, political and material ruin. Corruption dominates the ballot-box. . . . The people are demoralized; . . . The urban work[men] are denied the right to organize for self-protection, imported pauperized labor beats down their wages [and] . . . the fruits of the toils of millions are boldly stolen to build up colossal fortunes for a few, unprecedented in the history of mankind. . . . From the same prolific womb of governmental injustice we breed the two great classes: tramps and millionaires. . . .

Controlling influences dominating both . . . [the Republican and Democratic] parties have permitted the existing dreadful conditions to develop without serious effort to prevent or restrain them. Neither do they now promise any substantial reform. . . .

They propose to sacrifice our homes, lives, and children on the altar of mammon [money]; to destroy the multitude in order to secure corruption funds from the millionaires. . . .

We seek to restore the government of the Republic to the hands of the "plain people."

Source: American Social History Project, "The Omaha Platform: Launching the Populist Party," *History Matters: The U.S. Survey Course on the Web.* http://historymatters.gmu.edu/d/5361.

The Populist Party endorsed Democratic presidential candidate William Jennings Bryan in 1896.

Political corruption was another favorite target of the Populists. Leaders of the movement fought, for example, to reform the civil service so that government jobs would be filled by qualified workers rather than individuals with political connections. Populists also were pioneers in calling for direct election of representatives to Congress.

In 1891 the movement's leadership founded the Populist Party, a political party designed to provide American voters with an alternative to the Republicans and the Democrats. Over the next several years the party had candidates run for the White House and Congress, and in 1894 it even managed to claim six seats in the U.S. Senate. In 1896 the Populists decided to endorse Democratic presidential candidate William Jennings Bryan, who shared many of their political beliefs. Bryan lost to Republican William McKinley, though, and the Populist Party faded away over the next few years due to its failure to expand beyond its rural base.

Despite its short life span, though, many historians believe that the Populist movement helped shape the character of the Progressive movement of the early twentieth century. For example, progressivism in the South and Great Plains states, where populism had been strongest, focused most heavily on economic issues that affected farmers and rural communities. Other Progressives concentrated on urban poverty, child labor, and other "city" problems, while these agrarian Progressives aimed their fire at the predatory business practices of railroads, meat processors, and other industrial giants upon which farmers and ranchers relied for their livelihoods.

Labor activists and Populists were among the most vocal critics of American industrialization, but they did not stand alone. Many educated, middle-class Americans also felt outraged over the huge chasm between the nation's wealthy elite and the rest of its citizenry. They felt that this divide mocked American and Christian ideals of equality and compassion.

A Middle-Class Cause

During the age of industrialization the anger, frustration, and hopelessness felt by America's poor and working class had piled up into massive stacks of tinder. But the efforts of the Grangers and Populists and unions had failed to set this fuel ablaze and reform American society. It was not until America's middle class became engaged in the issues of poverty and corruption and social justice that the flickering fire of Progressive reform was transformed into a roaring inferno.

Some middle-class Americans joined the Progressive movement out of a desire to preserve their comfortable, privileged lifestyle. They believed that their idyllic middle-class existence might be threatened if America did not implement reforms to address its festering problems of poverty, corruption, and class division. They reasoned that if moderate reforms to address the worst corporate abuses and slum conditions were passed, the radical voices preaching revolution would fade away. They would be able to sleep soundly, secure in the knowledge that their stable daily lives would be there for them when they woke up.

Many other middle-class Americans, however, joined the Progressive movement out of a genuine sense of moral obligation to the poor. Most members of the American middle class at the beginning of the twentieth century were native-born white families. Few immigrants, African Americans, and other minorities of this era possessed the financial and educational resources or social contacts to achieve a middle-class level of security and comfort. This state of affairs was seen as acceptable—and even desirable—by many white members of the middle class. But the belief that one had a moral duty to aid the less fortunate had been a bedrock principle of American society since colonial times, and it remained an important part of American self-identity.

This sense of moral responsibility was fed in large part by the strong religious beliefs of most middle-class families in America. The greed and avarice of the Gilded Age deeply offended these men and women, who had been raised on biblical themes that emphasized fellowship, community, and good works for the benefit of all God's children. By the start of the twentieth century, large segments of the nation's middle class were joining a so-called Social Gospel movement. This movement was based on the belief that it was time "to return to American life an emphasis on Protestant morals that had been lost in an economic system that worshipped mammon [money] more

than Christ. . . . Progressivism for such people became a mission, a holy war, a crusade for virtue and the betterment of mankind."[11]

As the twentieth century began, then, middle-class Americans had become "deeply stirred" by the problems confronting the nation, according to Kansas newspaper editor William Allen White. "Our sympathies were responding excitedly to a sense of injustice that had become a part of the new glittering, gaudy machine age," he wrote.

> Machines of steel and copper and wood and stone, and bookkeeping and managerial talent, were creating a new order. It looked glamorous. It seemed permanent; yet, because someway the masses of the world, not the proletariat but the middle class, had qualms and squeamish doubts about the way things were going, discontent rose in the hearts of the people.[12]

Early Government Reform Efforts

This widespread unhappiness with the state of American society forced U.S. lawmakers to pass several reform-minded laws in the 1880s and 1890s. The first major reform was the 1883 Pendleton Act, which was championed by Ohio senator George Hunt Pendleton. This law created the foundation for the modern civil service system by tearing down the spoils system that had held sway in American politics for more than half a century.

Under the spoils system, many government jobs had been filled by friends and supporters of politicians rather than by qualified applicants. The Pendleton Act did not end this practice, but it did eliminate some of the most corrupt elements of the spoils system. For example, the act provided for open exams for applicants for government jobs and made it illegal for lawmakers to force civil servants to help their political campaigns.

Other efforts at reform were not so successful, however. In 1887, for example, Congress created the Interstate Commerce Commission (ICC) to regulate the railroad industry. The arrival of the ICC was an important milestone because it was the nation's first federal regulatory agency. But the agency was given only limited power to enforce its rules, so some railroads continued to charge inflated freight rates and engage in other ruthless business practices.

Other laws meant to curb the power of America's corporate giants also proved ineffective. One famous example of this was the 1890 Sherman Antitrust Act, which was named for its chief sponsor, Republican senator John Sherman of Ohio. The law was meant to prevent a single trust, or related group of companies, from dominating a given industry, but it failed miserably. In 1895, for instance, federal authorities charged the American Sugar Refining Company with violating the act. But even though the company controlled 98 percent of the nation's sugar production at that time, the pro-business U.S. Supreme Court ruled in *U.S. v. E.C. Knight* that the act applied strictly to the sale of goods, not to the manufacturing or production of goods. After this ruling, neither government regulators nor corporations paid much attention to the act.[13]

Despite these disappointments, the thirst for genuine reform of American politics and business did not subside. Instead, the calls for reform became even greater in the 1890s. During this decade, Americans were rocked by a four-year economic depression that began in 1893. Their anxiety about the future was further heightened by bitter and sometimes violent labor disputes in numerous industries.

The Haymarket Tragedy

One particularly violent confrontation between workers and management during America's age of industrialization was Chicago's Haymarket Riot of 1886. The riot began on May 3, when owners of the McCormick Reaper Works convinced city leaders to use the municipal police to break local support of a nationwide strike that had been called two days earlier by union leaders seeking better wages and shorter work weeks. When the police arrived, they immediately clashed with striking workers and their supporters. The violence quickly spiraled to the point that officers fired into the crowd of protestors, killing several strikers.

One day later, a group of anarchists seized on public anger about the shootings and organized a protest meeting at Haymarket Square. When Chicago police arrived at the square to disperse the protestors, one anarchist threw a homemade bomb into their ranks. The explo-

The clash between labor and management resulted in tragedy during the Haymarket Riot of 1886.

sion killed seven officers and wounded twenty-seven others.

Eight anarchists were arrested and convicted of murder in the aftermath of the tragedy. Four of the convicted activists were executed, and another committed suicide in prison. Meanwhile, other labor leaders tried to disassociate themselves from the anarchists, who terrified mainstream Americans. Still, many workers, union activists, left-wing political radicals, and opponents of capital punishment asserted that the anarchists had been convicted on flimsy evidence, and in 1893 Illinois governor John Peter Altgeld pardoned the three surviving prisoners in the case.

The Pullman Strike

The most notorious of the labor-management clashes was the 1894 Pullman Strike in Chicago. This dispute started when the owners of the Pullman Palace Car Company sharply reduced employee wages—but made no changes to the rents they demanded for the company-owned homes in which the workers lived. The company also refused to drop the prices of goods at their company stores. Pullman workers were outraged. Labor organizer Eugene V. Debs, president of the American Railway Union, quickly organized the workers in a strike that spread to other railroads in the western half of the country. As railroad operations ground to a halt, railroad owners and businesses dependent on rail service asked the federal government to intervene. President Grover Cleveland ordered federal troops into Illinois. The strike was broken and Debs was arrested.

Many Americans approved of President Cleveland's intervention and sided with management in the Pullman dispute. But others were outraged by the events in Chicago. They interpreted the outcome of the Pullman Strike as clear evidence that hardworking but poor Americans remained no match for the powerful corporate giants holding the nation's economic and political levers.

As the final years of the nineteenth century ticked away, the calls for reform of America's economic, political, and social fabric became steadily louder. Even the rich and powerful industrialists who controlled the country's factories, shipyards, and railroads began to take notice of the rising clamor. They were troubled by a steady escalation in labor disputes across the country, as well as growing public anxiety about poverty, urban squalor, and political corruption. Some men, such as famed attorney Clarence Darrow, even warned them that ugly class divisions in America threatened the very existence of the country. "If [the country's collapse] shall come in the lightning and tornado of civil war, the same as forty years ago," said Darrow in 1895, "when you then look over the ruin and desolation, remember the long years

In 1894 striking railway workers fought for fair wages during the Pullman Strike. President Grover Cleveland finally intervened and forced the railway workers back on the job.

John D. Rockefeller and Standard Oil

The richest man in America during the Progressive Era was industrialist John D. Rockefeller (1839–1937). Born in upstate New York in July 1839, Rockefeller became an investor and speculator in the oil industry in the 1860s, and in 1870 he established the Standard Oil Company. Over the next several years Rockefeller used secret alliances with other powerful businessmen in the railroad and oil industries to force dozens of other refiners to sell their operations to him or go out of business.

In 1882 Rockefeller formed the Standard Oil Trust, which accounted for more than 90 percent of the oil refined in the United States. By the end of the 1890s Standard dominated all phases of the oil industry—exploration, refining, and marketing—and Rockefeller's creation was the richest and most feared company in America.

In 1906 President Theodore Roosevelt declared war on the Standard Oil Trust and its stranglehold over the oil industry. Charging Rockefeller and Standard with a wide range of unfair and illegal business practices, Roosevelt moved to break the trust into smaller independent companies. Rockefeller fought back in the courts, but in May 1911 the U.S. Supreme Court ruled against him. By the end of the year, Standard Oil had been dismantled into several smaller—but still powerful—companies.

For much of his business career, Rockefeller was hated by the American public for his ruthless ways. In the 1910s and 1920s, though, his generous philanthropic gifts in the areas of education, art, and scientific research made him more popular.

Source: Ron Chernow, *Titan: The Life of John D. Rockefeller, Sr.* New York: Random House, 1998.

John D. Rockefeller.

in which the storm was rising, and do not blame the thunderbolt."[14]

As America's industrialists and politicians assessed the severity of the gathering threat, the most sensible of them heeded Darrow's words. They remembered the 1870s, 1880s, and 1890s, when a wide range of political reformers and radicals had raged against the abuses of industrial America. Back then, the corporations had ruthlessly used their political connections and economic might to neutralize the early reformers—Grangers, Populists, Socialists, and unionists—who tried to bring about major, lasting changes to American laws and society. But as the nineteenth century drew to a close, a new generation of reformers rose to carry on their campaigns of social and economic justice. These activists were far more influential than the Grangers, Populists, and early unionists had ever been. Shaken by this knowledge, some industrialists and lawmakers decided that they needed to make some changes if they hoped to keep Darrow's grim warning from coming true.

Chapter Two

Social and Political Reforms of the Progressive Era

During the opening years of the twentieth century, the Progressive movement transformed American society in many important ways. Social problems such as poverty, political corruption, unequal rights for women, alcohol abuse, and exploitation of children and immigrants ranked as primary targets of reformers. But another long-standing problem in America—discrimination and violence against African Americans and other minorities—did not receive the same attention. In fact, many Progressives embraced segregation as the best way to address the nation's troubled race relations. This decision stands as perhaps the single greatest stain on the legacy of the Progressive Era.

Explosive Growth in the Cities

The industrial revolution changed the United States from a society of farmers and rural towns to one of factory workers and sprawling cities. Agriculture was still important to the economy, and millions of families continued to support themselves by raising crops or livestock even after the nineteenth-century emergence of the railroad, telegraph, textile factory, and steel foundry. With each passing decade, though, the percentage of Americans who lived in cities—where the industrial jobs were located—grew larger.

At the beginning of the twentieth century, the nation's sixty largest cities housed about 28 million Americans, around 37 percent of the total population. Thirty years later, over 59 million people lived in these cities, about half of the total U.S. population. The dramatic growth of America's cities came from two places: the migration of citizens from rural to urban areas, and the arrival of immigrants from overseas.

In terms of migration within the United States, both native-born blacks and native-born whites were attracted to the industrial jobs that the cities offered. Northern cities such as New York, Cleveland, Chicago, Detroit, and Philadelphia, which had become centers of industry, were particularly popular destinations. The city lights of the North held the possibility of a better life for poor rural whites, but they shone even brighter for African Americans in the South. Black southerners had endured decades of poverty and humiliation as a result of discriminatory "Jim Crow" laws in the South, and they were anxious to escape. "As long as Jim Crow ruled the South, that system of segregation, subordination, and terror created powerful incentives for leaving and staying away."[15] The first great migratory wave of rural southern blacks to the industrial cities of the North began in the 1890s, and these waves became more powerful in each of the next three decades.

The movement from rural America to the great industrial cities occurred at the same time that foreign immigrants were entering the United States in greater numbers than ever before. During much of the nineteenth century, most immigrants came from the western European nations of England, Ireland, Germany, and Scandinavia. At the end of the century and during the first years of the 1900s, though, the great majority of immigrants came from eastern and southern Europe. Many of these immigrants

In the early 1900s, the majority of immigrants to the United States came from eastern and southern Europe.

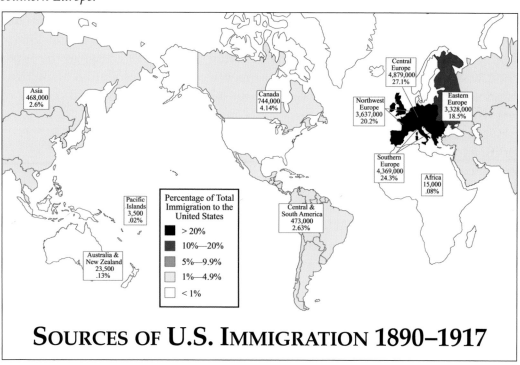

SOURCES OF U.S. IMMIGRATION 1890–1917

settled in ethnic enclaves in the cities. Surrounded by neighbors with the same cultural backgrounds as themselves, these newcomers could practice their religions, speak their native languages, and engage in other ethnic traditions in relative peace.

Life in the City

The new arrivals to the industrial cities provided essential labor for factories, stockyards, construction companies, and other industries. But the urban conditions in which most of these workers lived and toiled were terrible. American cities simply did not have the capacity to keep up with the population explosions they were experiencing. One historian, for example, points out that in 1840, "Chicago had been a village of log huts around Fort Dearborn holding scarcely five thousand residents; by 1890, it was a city of 165 square miles with one million residents, increasing by some fifty thousand each year, transforming pastures seemingly overnight into swarming tenements."[16]

Overcrowding reached epidemic proportions in every large city. Families crammed together in tenement slums that became breeding grounds for disease and crime. Factories and municipal sewage systems, meanwhile, dumped horrifying amounts of pollution into the air and water because there were virtually no laws against such practices. Residents became accustomed to these wretched living conditions, but they stunned visitors. Author Hamlin Garland wrote that the memory of his first glimpse of turn-of-the-century Chicago would always haunt him: "[I shall] never forget the feeling of dismay with which . . . I perceived from the [rail] car window a huge smoke-cloud which embraced the whole eastern horizon, for this, I was told, was the soaring banner of the great and gloomy inland metropolis."[17]

The poor living conditions in working-class neighborhoods tormented fathers and mothers who had hoped to provide better lives for their families. But unskilled and semiskilled industrial workers were paid such meager wages that they had little hope of securing better accommodations elsewhere in the city, let alone out in the comparatively safe, spacious, and comfortable suburbs. In fact, the challenge of economic survival was so great that many families had to rely on a household economy in which all family members worked. Millions of families were forced to send their children to work in factories at shockingly young ages. By the close of the nineteenth century, exploitation of children for labor was a widespread feature of America's industrial cities.

Political Machines and Political Reform

All of these problems were aggravated by the political corruption that wracked virtually every large municipal government. Fraud, bribery, and other profit-making activities were so commonplace in city governments that officials and residents alike came to see the corruption as the usual state of affairs. Lawmakers and officials claimed that their acceptance of bribes and doling out of political

At the turn of the twentieth century, the extremely low wages paid to unskilled factory workers forced many families to live in crowded, unsafe conditions.

Jane Addams and the Settlement-House Movement

Hull House founder Jane Addams was born in Cedarville, Illinois, on September 6, 1860. Raised in comfortable surroundings by parents who taught tolerance and compassion for others, Addams decided to open a settlement house in Chicago after touring similar facilities in Europe. She and fellow Progressive activist Ellen Gates Starr founded Hull House on Chicago's West Side in 1889, and over the next two decades it became the nation's most famous private provider of social programs for poor and working-class families. It also became the blueprint for the hundreds of other settlement houses that sprang up in American cities during the Progressive Era.

The fame of Hull House vaulted Addams into a position of national prominence. Addams wrote numerous books explaining her Progressive ideals, and she went on lecture tours around the country to talk about the settlement-house movement. She also served in leadership positions in important reform organizations such as the Consumers League, the National Conference of Charities and Corrections, and the National Child Labor Committee. She also spoke out on behalf of woman suffrage and assisted in the founding of the National Association for the Advancement of Colored People (NAACP) in 1909 and the American Civil Liberties Union in 1920.

A dedicated pacifist, Addams strongly opposed U.S. entry into World War I. In 1919 she was elected first president of the Women's International League for Peace and Freedom, an organization dedicated to international peace efforts. Her work in this area, though, led critics to accuse her of disloyalty and Communist political beliefs. Undaunted, Addams remained an energetic peace activist and social reformer. In 1931 she was awarded the Nobel Peace Prize for her many works. She died in Chicago on May 21, 1935.

Source: Jean Bethke Elshtain, *Jane Addams and the Dream of American Democracy: A Life*. New York: Basic Books, 2001.

Jane Addams

favors was nothing more than "honest graft," and many residents accepted the existence of corrupt political parties and government agencies because their influence seemed too powerful to resist.

In the Progressive Era, though, these machines came under sustained attack. Investigations of fraud and bribery increased, and some cities passed important reforms to improve the performance and responsiveness of municipal agencies.

City governments were by no means the only focus of political reform. Corruption at the state and federal level was also a terrible problem. Progressives acted decisively in this area as well. Reform-minded governors like Hiram Johnson of California and Robert M. La Follette of Wisconsin promoted wider citizen participation in the electoral process. They knew that if ordinary citizens received a greater voice in selecting their representatives and making laws, the influence of powerful corporate interests and corrupt lawmakers would be reduced.

Efforts to usher in a new era of direct democracy included the introduction of the initiative, the recall, the referendum, and the primary into American politics. Many of these measures were first approved in western states and gradually moved eastward. The initiative gave voters the power to pass legislation on their own in special elections, rather than depend on corrupt, incompetent, or hostile lawmakers. This became an important tool of the Prohibition and Suffrage movements in the 1900s and 1910s. The recall allowed voters to remove elected officials from office in special elections.

The referendum gave voters the power to repeal laws that they did not like. And the primary neutralized the power of political machines by taking the selection of political candidates out of the hands of party leaders and placing it into the hands of voting citizens.

The Progressive campaign to reduce corruption and backroom dealing even extended to the way that United States senators were elected. For more than a century, U.S. senators had been elected or appointed by state legislatures rather than by popular vote. Progressives changed this by successfully campaigning for a constitutional amendment that would provide for the direct election of senators by the people. This amendment—the Seventeenth Amendment to the Constitution—was ratified by the states on April 8, 1913, and was first put into effect for the 1914 elections.

Muckrakers in the Cities

The early leaders in these crusades to address America's massive urban problems were Progressive reformers who were often affiliated with churches and private charities. Their efforts to enlist the support of middle-class Americans in their cause were greatly aided by two factors. One factor was the growing belief within middle-class homes and neighborhoods that corporate exploitation of workers had to be curbed, and poor Americans deserved a helping hand. The other factor—which played a major role in shaping middle-class opinion—was the muckraking work of newspaper and magazine journalists.

American magazines and newspapers reached the historical height of their power during the Progressive Era. They were the primary source of news in this pre-television and pre-Internet age, and revolutionary innovations in transportation and communication during the second half of the 1800s gave them greater reach than they had ever enjoyed before. Many of these magazines and newspapers were led by Progressives, and they supported journalists who relentlessly exposed the seamy underside of America's industrial progress. Crusading journalists such as Henry Demarest Lloyd, Ray Stannard Baker, Ida Tarbell, Charles Edward Russell, Frank Norris, David Graham Phillips, and Lincoln Steffens filled the pages of *Atlantic Monthly*, *McClure's*, *American Magazine*, *Cosmopolitan*, *Everybody's Magazine*, and other prominent publications with chilling accounts of corporate ruthlessness, urban hopelessness, and political corruption.

Book publishers added their voices as well. They printed important works such as *How the Other Half Lives* (1890), a book by reformer Jacob Riis that forced Americans to confront the wretched conditions in the urban slums. Other influential books included Steffens's *The Shame of the Cities* (1904), which revealed the corruption of city governments in New York and Chicago; Frank Norris's novel *The Octopus* (1901), which condemned greedy railroads; and Upton Sinclair's *The Jungle* (1906), which shocked Americans with its descriptions of the brutality and unhealthy conditions found in the nation's meatpacking industry.

These articles and books triggered numerous investigations of corrupt political and business interests. They also helped build public support for local, state, and federal laws designed to address the problems of child labor, hazardous working conditions, unsanitary and overcrowded slums, and exploited immigrants. In one case—Upton Sinclair's famous novel *The Jungle*—a muckraking work was directly responsible for the creation of two of the most important laws of the entire Age of Reform. The Pure Food and Drug Act and the Meat Inspection Act, both of which were signed into law by President Theodore Roosevelt in 1906, were created explicitly to address the outrage that Americans expressed after reading Sinclair's book.

Jane Addams and the Women Reformers

The works of America's muckraking journalists inspired the efforts of the larger Progressive movement that swept across the country during the first two decades of the twentieth century. Within this movement, educated white middle-class women were a particularly influential group. "They not only were strongly moved by the moral and ethical dilemmas of their time," explained one scholar, "but also found an outlet for their talents working among the poor that the broader society denied them."[18]

Seizing on the widespread belief that women were America's moral guardians and protectors of hearth and home, female reformers argued that they had an ethical

In his 1890 book How the Other Half Lives, *progressive journalist Jacob Riis showcased images such as the one pictured, which depicts children in American cities living in poverty.*

duty to make their voices heard on public sanitation, education, poverty, and other issues that affected families. Their message was embraced by other women, who joined the Progressive cause in huge numbers during the 1890s and the first decade of the twentieth century.

These women activists were responsible for creating and nurturing some of the country's most prominent reform-oriented associations. Organizations such as the Women's Trade Union League, the Women's Christian Temperance Union, and the National Consumers' League joined other Progressive organizations in crusades against a wide assortment of social ills, from alcohol abuse and sexual permissiveness to exploitation of women and children in the garment industry. Protestant ministers were a particularly important ally in these efforts. Troubled by the corruption and poverty of industrial America, they preached a Social Gospel message that called on church members to find salvation by reaching out to the less fortunate.

Women also were essential in the development and maintenance of settlement houses, which were designed to help immigrant families adjust to their bewildering new lives in America. The first of these facilities sprouted in American cities in the late 1880s and early 1890s. By 1910 more than four hundred settlement houses had been established in cities across the country. The settlement houses gave immigrants instruction on everything from housecleaning to civic responsibilities. Settlement house leaders also lobbied city and state officials to improve workplace safety, increase trash collection and expand sewage systems, eliminate child labor in urban factories, combat prostitution, and increase welfare benefits for widows, the elderly, and impoverished citizens.

The most famous of the nation's settlement houses was Chicago's Hull House, which was founded by Jane Addams in 1889. The model for many later settlement houses, Hull House provided services to the immigrant families that crowded the tenements of Chicago's West Side. As the Progressive movement gained strength, Addams and her female lieutenants at Hull House established an amazing array of social programs for working-class families that were not yet available from state or federal governments. These included kindergarten and day care facilities for the children of working mothers; an employment bureau; libraries and an art gallery; meeting places for trade unions; recreational activities for young single women; and classes in English, citizenship, music, art, and theater.

In many cases, the advocacy efforts of settlement house reformers made a real difference in people's lives. Settlement house activists, for example, were essential in convincing legislators to establish separate courts for juvenile offenders in twenty-two states and widows' pension programs in twenty states by the end of 1913.[19] Lillian Wald of New York's Henry Street Settlement House also was instrumental in the 1912 creation of the Federal Children's Bureau, the first federal agency charged with monitoring and investigating child labor in American industries. Addams, Wald, and other settlement house reformers also generated vital public and legislative support for the 1916 passage of the Keating-Owen Child Labor Act, the first federal law restricting child labor. It limited the working hours of children and forbade the interstate sale of goods produced by child labor.

Advancing Women's Rights

Women's rights were another major cause of the Progressives. In the areas of sexuality and marriage, some reformers turned their energies to abolishing pornography, ending prostitution, and raising the age of sexual consent. Others—especially women in the movement—fought for more sex education, greater sexual freedom for women, and increased social acceptance of divorce. The latter group of reformers were also in the forefront of the birth control movement. Advocates of birth control and legal abortion became a powerful political force in the 1910s under the leadership of Margaret Sanger, who in 1922 founded the organization that eventually became the pro-choice Planned Parenthood Federation of America.

Birth control was a controversial issue in America, but it was eclipsed during the Progressive Era by the issue of woman

One of the services provided by Chicago's Hull House was day care for working mothers.

Women's rights came to the forefront during the Progressive Era, especially in regard to women gaining the right to vote. Here, suffragettes march in New York City in 1912.

suffrage. The struggle to give women the right to vote had been waged since 1848, when Lucretia Mott and Elizabeth Cady Stanton organized the first woman suffrage convention in New York. But the movement enjoyed little success until the beginning of the twentieth century, when woman suffrage received a huge boost from Progressives who believed that women could provide the necessary votes to pass Progressive legislation.

By 1910 seven western states had given women the right to vote, in part because of the support of prominent men such as Democratic senator Robert Owen of Oklahoma and the Progressive Kansas newspaper editor William Allen White. Two years later, former president Theodore Roosevelt—the great political hero of the entire Progressive Era—abandoned his previous cautious support for woman suffrage. As the presidential nominee of the Progressive or Bull Moose Party, he enthusiastically endorsed the idea. His 1912 campaign to reclaim the White House failed, but Roosevelt and the Progressive Party became the first major American political party to welcome women as equals. Women were placed in leadership positions in the party and played important roles in the campaign, and Jane Addams even received the honor of seconding Roosevelt's nomination at the party convention.

In the mid-1910s divisions within the suffrage movement threatened to derail the quest to secure voting rights for all adult women citizens across America. But the militant protests of woman suffrage advocates like Alice Paul kept the issue alive. "To me it was shocking that a government of men could look with such extreme contempt on a movement that was asking nothing except such a simple little thing as the right to vote,"[20] Paul later recalled. Paul and other suffragettes waged a relentless campaign of demonstrations, hunger strikes, and picketing outside the White House in the hope of getting President Woodrow Wilson to drop his neutral stance on the issue. This continued pressure, combined with the steady efforts of more moderate groups like the National American Woman Suffrage Association (NAWSA), finally convinced the Wilson administration to endorse woman suffrage.

Wilson's support for suffrage had an immediate impact on Congress, which had previously done its best to ignore the issue. On May 21, 1919, the Nineteenth Amendment to the U.S. Constitution granting women the right to vote (widely known as the Susan B. Anthony Amendment) passed the U.S. House of Representatives. Two weeks later, on June 4, the measure passed the U.S. Senate and went to the states for ratification.

In Support of Women's Suffrage

One of the leading supporters of woman suffrage in the U.S. Senate was Oklahoma's Robert Owen, a Progressive Democrat. Following is an excerpt from a 1910 speech Owen delivered in which he highlighted the benefits of suffrage in western states that had passed suffrage laws:

The man is usually better informed with regard to state government, but women are better informed about house government, and she can learn state government with as much facility as he can learn how to instruct children, properly feed and clothe the household, care for the sick, play on the piano, or make a house beautiful. . . .

Every evil prophecy against granting the suffrage has failed. The public men of Colorado, Wyoming, Utah, and Idaho give it a cordial support. The testimony is universal: . . . It has made women broader and greatly increased the understanding of the community at large of the problems of good government; of proper sanitation, of pure food, or clean water, and all such matters in which intelligent women would naturally take an interest. It has not absolutely regenerated society, but it has improved it.

Source: *Annals of the American Academy of Political and Social Science* 35 (Supplement), May 1910, pp. 6–9.

If approved by three-fourths of the states—a total of thirty-six at that time—the proposed amendment would become law. Legislatures in Michigan and Wisconsin were the first to ratify the amendment, and in the ensuing months many other states followed suit. Finally, on August 26, 1920, Tennessee became the thirty-sixth state to ratify the amendment. After years of struggle and disappointment, American women finally had the right to vote.

The War on Alcohol

Some Progressives also joined the long and bitter war against alcohol consumption in American society. Not all Progressives supported campaigns for temperance (moderate use of alcohol) or outright bans or prohibitions on alcohol production and consumption. Those who did support these measures, though, believed that alcohol abuse made life worse for countless families, especially in the poor tenement neighborhoods of the big cities. Some prohibition activists even saw alcohol as a mortal threat to the future of the nation. As one Presbyterian minister stated, "[Liquor is] the open sore of this land . . . the most fiendish, corrupt and hell-soaked institution that ever crawled out of the slime of the eternal pit."[21]

America's leading antialcohol groups, such as the Women's Christian Temperance Union (WCTU) and the Anti-Saloon League, had been founded in the 1870s and 1880s. But despite the efforts of early prohibition leaders like Frances Willard, Carry Nation, and Howard Hyde Russell, they made little progress until the late 1890s. At this time public anxiety about immigrants, chaotic cities, and a long economic depression brought new supporters into the fold. "If cities were choking in industrial smoke and shameful immorality, if strange new peoples and alien languages and political philosophies cast an eerie cloud over traditional America, there had to be reasons," explained one scholar. "If economic misery strangled the nation, if families split apart, if crime increased and suicides were on the rise, there had to be answers. For many the greatest of the reasons was liquor; the most urgent of the answers was to wipe it out."[22] Christian evangelist Billy Sunday, one of the most famous prohibition champions of the Progressive Era, summed up this view in his famous "Booze Sermon": "The saloon is the sum of all villainies. It is worse than war or pestilence. . . . It is the parent of crimes and the mother of sins."[23]

At the outset of the twentieth century, only Kansas, Maine, and North Dakota had passed statewide bans on alcohol. But from 1907 to 1909, six southern states enacted prohibition laws despite opposition from liquor producers, liquor distributors, and working-class Americans who resented being lectured about how they spent their few leisure hours.

Efforts to pass national prohibition laws also gained additional support due to the tireless efforts of Sunday and Anti-Saloon League leaders like Wayne Wheeler, Bishop James Cannon Jr., and Purley A. Baker. "The vices of the cities have been the undoing of past empires and civilizations," declared Baker in

Members of the Women's Christian Temperance Union march in Washington, D.C., in 1909 to support a national ban on alcohol.

1914. "The saloon stands for the worst in political life. All who stand for the best must be aggressively against it. If our Republic is to be saved the liquor traffic must be destroyed."[24]

Politicians, though, remained wary of voicing support for prohibition, even though it was popular with large numbers of both evangelicals and Progressives. The beer, wine, and liquor industries were important sources of campaign contributions for many local and state politicians. Even politicians holding national office recognized that prohibition was deeply unpopular with significant numbers of American voters. All three presidents of the Progressive Era—Theodore Roosevelt, William Taft, and Woodrow Wilson—tried to avoid taking any stance at all on the issue. "My experience with prohibitionists," admitted Roosevelt, "is . . . that the best way to deal with them is to ignore them."[25]

The Age of Prohibition

In the 1910s, though, the political power of the prohibition movement became clear to all. Sweeping new laws were passed against alcohol in nine states, and many legislators who opposed prohibition were voted out of office across the country. Lawmakers in Washington, D.C., responded quickly to the shift in momentum. In 1917 Congress passed a proposed constitutional amendment prohibiting the manufacture, distribution, or sale of alcoholic beverages. It then sent it to the individual states for ratification. On January 8, 1918, Mississippi was the first state to ratify the proposed amendment. One year later Nebraska became the thirty-sixth state to do so. On January 16, 1919, the prohibition amendment officially became the Eighteenth Amendment to the U.S. Constitution. On January 17, 1920, Prohibition took effect across the land.

Advocates of Prohibition rejoiced at their victory, but enforcement of the new law was an utter failure from the start. An underground industry devoted to providing alcohol to thirsty Americans sprang up virtually overnight. By the mid-1920s huge numbers of illegal drinking establishments—known as speakeasies and blind pigs—could be found in every American city. These establishments ranged from glamorous clubs with live entertainment to filthy barrooms with a few scattered tables. Some were managed by organized crime syndicates, which achieved new levels of power from the bootlegging trade.

By the end of the Roaring Twenties—a post–World War I era of American pleasure-seeking and economic prosperity—Prohibition was in tatters. In 1929 Mabel Walker Willebrandt, who was the Justice Department's director of Prohibition enforcement, bluntly admitted that huge quantities of inexpensive liquor were being consumed all across the country in rural hamlets and big cities alike.

The stock market crash of October 1929 and the Great Depression that followed brought the Prohibition era to a close. Americans of all political orientations argued that ending Prohibition would boost the sputtering economy and help the government focus its energies on more pressing troubles. In February 1933 a resolution calling for repeal of the Eighteenth Amendment passed Congress and was sent to the states for ratification. In just ten months, thiry-five of the necessary thirty-six states approved the amendment. When Utah became the thiry-sixth state to ratify the measure on December 5, 1933, the Twenty-First Amendment to the U.S. Constitution came into effect, and the Prohibition era formally came to an end.

Progressives and Segregation

Another social problem that Progressives tried to address was racial turmoil in America. But instead of calling for equal rights for African Americans and other minorities, Progressives turned to segregation as the best policy for reducing racial violence and defusing the racial tensions that were shaking American society.

During the Prohibition years, illegal alcohol still found its way into every big city across the nation.

In the South, formal laws and unwritten rules called Jim Crow laws denied African Americans access to many southern restaurants, hotels, theaters, pool halls, and swimming pools. Jim Crow laws also forced African Americans to accept inferior accommodations in public streetcars, theaters, schools, trains, and restrooms. Despite this strict segregation, however, the threat of racial violence hovered over every black family in the South. In fact, vicious white-on-black violence was a daily reality of the Jim Crow South.

Segregation policies, which kept African Americans in an inferior position in American society, went unchallenged by Progressive reformers.

Children in the Mines

In 1906 muckraking journalist John Spargo published The Bitter Cry of the Children, *which documented the problem of child labor in America in grim detail. The following excerpt from Spargo's book describes the lives of boys who worked in West Virginia's coal mines:*

The coal is hard, and accidents to the hands, such as cut, broken, or crushed fingers, are common among the boys. Sometimes there is a worse accident: a terrified shriek is heard, and a boy is mangled and torn in the machinery, or disappears in the chute to be picked out later smothered and dead. Clouds of dust fill the breakers [machines used to separate coal from other minerals] and are inhaled by the boys, laying the foundations for asthma and miners' consumption.

I once stood in a breaker for half an hour and tried to do the work a twelve-year-old boy was doing day after day, for ten hours at a stretch, for sixty cents a day. The gloom of the breaker appalled me. Outside the sun shone brightly . . . and the birds sang in chorus with the trees and the rivers. Within the breaker there was blackness, clouds of deadly dust enfolded everything, the harsh, grinding roar of the machinery and the ceaseless rushing of coal through the chutes filled the ears. . . . I was covered from head to foot with coal dust, and for many hours afterwards I was expectorating [coughing up] some of the small particles of anthracite I had swallowed.

Source: John Spargo, *The Bitter Cry of the Children.* New York: Macmillan, 1906, pp. 163–65.

A group of young boys, known as Breaker Boys, after their shift at a Pennsylvania coal company.

Conditions in the North were better for African Americans, but only by comparison. Residential segregation was commonplace in northern cities, and educational and employment opportunities in the North remained much better for whites than for blacks.

Progressives wanted to bring an end to the lynchings and terrorization of African Americans, and they genuinely wanted to help improve the lives of blacks. But few of them subscribed to the words of Progressive journalist William English Walling, who declared that "we must come to treat the negro on a plane of absolute political and social equality."[26] Most white Progressives—North and South—believed that whites were intellectually and morally superior to other races. This included leading reform voices ranging from Roosevelt to Protestant minister Josiah Strong, a founder of the Social Gospel movement. Their goal, then, was to stabilize race relations by stamping out racial violence—not to lift African Americans to the same social and legal status as whites.

This attitude angered and frustrated early twentieth-century African American civil rights activists such as W.E.B. DuBois and Monroe Trotter. They condemned segregation as a moral outrage that cast a dark shadow over America's stated ideals of democracy and fairness. But racial prejudices were difficult to overcome, and all three presidents of the Progressive Era—Roosevelt, Taft, and Wilson—decided that their hopes of making other social, economic, and political reforms would be much greater if they did not alienate southern lawmakers who vowed to preserve segregation at all costs. As a result, segregation actually became even more firmly entrenched in American society during the first two decades of the twentieth century.

The reformers' support for segregation is now widely regarded as the most shameful chapter of the entire Progressive Era. "Segregation was . . . a failure of imagination and nerve," concluded one scholar.

The rise of progressivism represented a remarkable reworking of middle-class ideology, a creative deployment of a host of devises for reform, and a bold determination to take on some of the most basic and intractable issues of human existence. Willing to believe that a kind of "paradise" might really be attainable some day, Progressives showed little fear in dealing with problems of gender, family, class, and economy—but not of race."[27]

Chapter Three

Business and Labor Reforms of the Progressive Era

As the Progressive Era unfolded, reformers took significant steps to reduce the power of corporations over American workers and the wider American society. These efforts by presidents, legislators, labor leaders, and reform-minded activists succeeded in eliminating many of the worst corporate abuses that had afflicted the nation during the industrial revolution of the nineteenth century. But life in working-class America remained a struggle, at least partly because differing priorities kept the labor movement and the Progressive movement from establishing an enduring and powerful alliance.

Workers at the Mercy of Employers

In 1900 about 24 million people—one-third of the nation's population of 76 million—made up the country's active work force. The majority of these men, women, and children toiled with their hands on docks, roads, and farms, in factories, mines, and other people's houses. They practiced ancient crafts such as tailoring and carpentry, and newer arts such as iron molding and metal cutting. They were machine tenders in mills and factories, unskilled laborers in towns, farm hands in the countryside, cowboys on the range, and domestic servants. All of them, even the best-paid skilled workers, lived circumscribed, vulnerable lives, constrained by low pay and limited opportunity, and menaced by unemployment, ill health, and premature death.[28]

Workers in manufacturing industries, for example, earned an average of only $435 per year in 1900. Under this level of compensation, workers struggled mightily to provide their families with decent

As American families struggled to make ends meet, millions of children entered the work force so they could contribute to the household income.

shelter, clothing, and food. Laborers in the anthracite coal mining industry, one of the most dangerous industries in the nation, earned even less—about $340 a year on average. Farmhands and other agricultural workers, meanwhile, earned less than $180 annually, although they also received room and board.[29] Many unskilled and semiskilled workers also knew that their jobs might be lost at any time due to seasonal lulls, breakdowns of factory machinery, or shortages of raw materials necessary for production.

American workers who managed to secure steady work, meanwhile, often faced the grim prospect of crippling injury or even death. "Every working-class occupation had its difficulties and dangers, from the explosions, fires, cave-ins, debilitating 'miner's lung,' and other notorious perils of hard-rock mining in the West to the . . . asthma, byssinosis, tuberculosis, and maimings in the textile mills of the East."[30] In 1900 alone, for example, 1,500 American coal miners lost their lives on the job.[31] An even greater number of workers in the railroad industry—2,550 employees—died on the job that same year.[32]

The conditions in which American workers toiled also took a tremendous toll on their morale. The men who fed coal to the roaring furnaces of the eastern steel foundries, slaughtered livestock in the filthy slaughterhouses of the Midwest, and hacked through the bowels of the earth in search of western silver, copper, and other minerals went home dirty and exhausted day after day for years on end. Women and children were not spared, either. Millions suffered under grueling work conditions in steaming farm fields and on stifling factory floors. Women and children employed by textile manufacturing plants, for example, toiled six days a week, fourteen hours a day, in

> overheated, poorly ventilated room[s] that filled an entire floor. . . . Screeching, clanking pulleys and levers and wheels roared with a deafening clatter; vibrations from the top-floor looms shook walls, ceilings and floors as thousands of spring-loaded wood shuttles slammed against the side frames of looms, then back across at lightning speeds; they rattled and hammered without pause. . . . For some young women fresh off the farms of northern New England, most between the ages of sixteen and twenty-one, nothing but the absence of bars on windows distinguished these cotton factories from prisons.[33]

Finally, many workers in mining and other industries found themselves living in company towns—villages or towns in which most or all of the homes, stores, schools, hotels, hospitals, and other facilities were owned by a corporate employer. These towns were typically built up around the steel mill, coal mine, cannery, or factory at which the workers toiled. Many other municipalities, meanwhile, were not actually corporate-owned, but one employer provided so many jobs that its owners and managers were, for all practical purposes, the "bosses" of the entire town.

Not only did thousands of American workers toil long hours for little pay, but they often endured dangerous working conditions as well.

Some workers and their families favored the stability that some of these towns offered, but others chafed under the arrangement. They complained that it made them feel like dependent children or medieval serfs. As one worker for the Pullman Palace Car Company stated, "we are born in a Pullman house, fed from the Pullman shop, taught in the Pullman school, catechized in the Pullman church, and when we die we shall be buried in the Pullman cemetery and go to the Pullman hell."[34]

Unionization in America

By the time America sat poised to enter the twentieth century, unions added their collective voice to the growing demand for major social and economic reforms. Unions had actually been a fact of American life since the early 1800s. The first unions were early tradesmen associations. These associations were composed of skilled craftsmen, and they played an important role in lifting the economic fortunes of carpenters, printers, machinists, glassmakers, and other workers with specialized skills.

Union leaders bargained on behalf of members with employers on a wide range of issues, including wages, work hours, work rules, benefits, workplace safety, promotions, and other policies. By the 1850s craftsmen's organizations such as the International Typographical Union had achieved nationwide reach. During the 1860s and 1870s they managed to lift many of their members into the ranks of the American middle class. By the late nineteenth century the craft labor unions claimed nearly 10 percent of the total American workforce. The largest of these was the national American Federation of Labor (AFL), an association of thirteen craft unions headed by Samuel Gompers.

The picture was far bleaker, though, for most of America's unskilled and semi-skilled laborers. The workers who toiled over the assembly lines of New England's textile plants or spent their days scouring coal, gold, or copper out of the mountains of the West had virtually no bargaining power. They were at the mercy of the owners and managers of the great steel mills, mining companies, textile factories, and railroads of the industrial age.

The Courts' Biggest Weapon

American judges were frequently condemned by Progressives for excessive interference in labor-management disputes. Reformers and labor activists expressed particular fury with the judges' frequent use of injunctions—court orders—to cripple labor strikes or boycotts against corporations. "The results were devastating" for unions, said one historian. "A judge could enjoin [command] thousands of workers at a time; he could tell them not to picket, not to march, not to meet, not to shout 'scab' at strikebreakers."

The use of injunctions rose each decade from the 1880s through the 1920s, to the great dismay of labor leaders. United Mine Workers president John Mitchell, for example, wrote that "no weapon has been used with such disastrous effect against trade unions as the injunction in labor disputes. . . . It is difficult to speak in measured tone or moderate language of the savagery and venom with which unions have been assailed by the injunction."

As frustration mounted, legislative allies of the labor movement vowed to disarm judges. But most attempts to limit the powers of judges in management-labor cases failed. This situation remained basically unchanged until 1931, when the Norris-LaGuardia Act was passed. This law placed significant new restrictions on judges' rights to impose injunctions in labor cases.

Sources: Michael McGerr, *A Fierce Discontent: The Rise and Fall of the Progressive Movement in America.* New York: Oxford University Press, 2005, pp. 143–44. John Mitchell, *Organized Labor: Its Problems, Purposes, and Ideals and the Present and Future of American Wage Earners.* Philadelphia: American Book and Bible House, 1903, p. 324.

The United Mine Workers of America, founded in 1890, became the first successful union of mass-production industrial workers in U.S. history.

Most of these employers were determined to squeeze as much profit as they could out of their operations. This meant keeping wages low and forcing workers to work at an exhausting pace in often dangerous conditions. As one scholarly work noted, "promiscuous use of untested chemicals and unregulated work environments gave rise to new deformities and illness [during the age of industrialization]. Each year, thousands were killed and maimed in America's notoriously unsafe work sites."[35]

Some unskilled workers looked to the craft unions for help. But the AFL and other established trade unions showed little interest in lending a hand to factory workers, farming laborers, and other unskilled workers. "The skilled workers looked down on the unskilled, many of whom were recent immigrants, seeing them not as allies against management but as a burden, likely to bring down their own wages."[36]

As time went on, though, some activists managed to organize unions for unskilled workers. The first national union founded to represent all types of workers was the National Labor Union, which was created in 1866. But it collapsed in less than a decade under the strain of a national economic depression and a disastrous attempt by its leadership to form a political party.

A far more successful effort to gather all kinds of workers under a union banner was the Knights of Labor, which was founded in 1869 in Philadelphia. The Knights' platform, which called for an end to child labor, the institution of an eight-hour workday, and better wages, was enormously popular with the nation's factory workers. By 1887 the Knights had organized a number of successful strikes and expanded its membership to more than 700,000 workers—including women and African American workers, who were shut out by the AFL and other unions.

The success of the Knights of Labor turned out to be short-lived. The union fell apart in the 1890s, doomed by bad strategic decisions, a prolonged economic depression, and growing public

Samuel Gompers and the AFL

During his long tenure as the president of the American Federation of Labor (AFL), Samuel Gompers became one of the most influential labor leaders in U.S. history. Born on January 27, 1850, Gompers immigrated to the United States from England with his family when he was thirteen years old. He learned the cigar-making trade from his father, and in the 1870s he became a leader of the Cigar Makers' International Union (CIU).

In 1886 the CIU united with a dozen other trade unions to form the AFL. Gompers was the first president of the AFL, and with the exception of one year (1895) he headed the union until his death in 1924. Gompers focused on organizing trade workers with specialized knowledge and skills, rather than unskilled factory workers, whose labor could be replaced by strikebreakers. This approach angered other labor activists, who accused Gompers of building an "aristocracy of labor" at the AFL. But Gompers's strategy was successful. Membership in the AFL reached 2.86 million by the time of his death on December 13, 1924.

Throughout his tenure, Gompers avoided the radical political activism and confrontational tactics that marked other unions. He focused on "bread and butter" issues like wages, workplace safety, and shorter workdays. The labor agreements that he and his lieutenants negotiated with industry helped many AFL members gain greater economic and job security than American workers had ever enjoyed before.

Source: Melvyn Dubofsky and Foster Rhea Dulles. *Labor in America: A History,* 7th ed. Wheeling, IL: Harlan Davidson, 2004.

anxiety about the violence that swirled around many labor-management clashes of the era. But during this same period, two other unions were founded, and these organizations—the United Mine Workers (UMW) and the Industrial Workers of the World (IWW)—had an enormous impact on labor-management relations during the Progressive Era.

After its founding in 1890, the United Mine Workers became the first successful union of mass-production industrial workers in American history. It struggled in its first years, but in the late 1890s and early 1900s its president, John Mitchell, orchestrated several successful strikes against mine owners.

The second major labor union to emerge at the dawn of the twentieth century was the Industrial Workers of the World (commonly known as "Wobblies"). The IWW's membership never numbered more than 100,000, but the organization had a huge impact on labor-management relations and wider American society.

The "Wobblies"

When the IWW was founded in 1905, it vowed "no compromise and no surrender" in its quest to "confederate the workers of this country into a working class movement that shall have for its purpose the emancipation of the working class."[37] This attitude had been forged in the brutal mining camps of the West, where IWW leaders William "Big Bill" Haywood and Mary Harris "Mother" Jones had witnessed firsthand how mine owners used terror and violence to suppress union activities.

In the years following its founding, the Wobblies had a mixed influence on the Progressive Era. On the one hand, most Americans opposed their radical philosophy, which called for tearing down American society and building a new one that reflected Socialist ideals. Corporate interests took advantage of this hostility to the IWW by repeatedly trying to link *all* labor activists and rebellious unions to the Wobblies. These efforts were effective in delaying some workplace reforms and stoking public distrust of unions.

But the IWW also advanced the cause of the American worker in some ways. The organization's inclusion of women and African Americans was an important step in the development of the American labor movement. In addition, other labor groups embraced the confrontational tactics used by the Wobblies, and their dedication to their principles inspired other working men and women. Finally, the radicalism of the IWW and similar groups of that era convinced some of the power brokers in America's corporate boardrooms and statehouses that *some* compromises had to be made with the nation's angry industrial workers. Otherwise, they believed that the revolution for which the IWW campaigned might actually become a reality.

The dawning of the Progressive Era, though, brought big changes to the American labor movement. The era was not without its disappointments for union activists and labor members. For instance, union membership did not increase dramatically from 1900 to 1915, and some of

Unlike many other groups of the Progressive Era, the Industrial Workers of the World welcomed women and African Americans into its ranks.

the labor movement's most famous strikes and boycotts of these years ended in failure or tragedy. Nonetheless, millions of working men and women across America earned significantly higher wages, worked fewer hours, and enjoyed a better quality of life than only a few short years before. Scholars credit many of these gains to the awkward but effective alliance that labor leaders forged with Progressive reformers.

Progressives and Unions

Progressives were generally sympathetic to the struggles that working-class Americans faced in the new industrial age. As a result, they voiced support for the bargaining efforts of the AFL and other labor organizations that focused on basic issues like higher pay and workplace safety. Middle-class reformers believed that these sorts of gains would reduce the class divisions that were causing so

much turmoil in American society and bring a greater measure of stability and peace to the nation as a whole.

But many middle-class Progressives disliked and distrusted the more radical labor groups, such as the International Workers of the World (IWW). They saw the IWW and other confrontational organizations as a threat to the stable, unselfish, and morally upright country that they were trying to build. The famous Progressive activist Jane Addams, for example, declared that "a moral revolution cannot be accomplished by men who are held together merely because they are all smarting under a sense of injury and injustice."[38]

Progressives also voiced frustration with some of the labor movement's policies and priorities. The AFL and most other unions, for example, restricted or banned women from membership. Even women who formed their own unions

Progressives were sympathetic to the struggles that working-class Americans faced, and supported the bargaining efforts of labor organizations that focused on basic issues like higher pay and workplace safety.

were not shielded from glaring gender discrimination.

After the Women's Trade Union League was founded in 1903 it swore allegiance to Gompers's AFL, only to have the AFL leadership ignore the group and its issues. Women activists who were fighting for what they called "bread and roses"—"bread" referring to basic economic rights and security, and "roses" meaning dignity and hope for themselves and their children—became angered by this condescending and unfriendly attitude.

This attitude hurt the labor cause with the larger Progressive movement. Many Progressives were women who supported suffrage. Male Progressives also supported increased women's rights, including the right to vote. To these Americans, the behavior of the AFL and other male-dominated unions toward women was insulting and unfair.

Even so, Progressives and mainstream labor groups were able to find common ground in many areas. Both movements fought hard to reduce child labor in America, and they supported each other's efforts to pass new laws protecting working women. But the motivations that drove these groups to unite were somewhat different.

Progressives crusaded against corporate exploitation of women and children on moral grounds. Labor unions also saw these corporate abuses as immoral and evil, and they battled them for that reason. But they also worked to pass business reform laws in these areas because they knew that such laws would increase the demand for—and thus the bargaining power of—their overwhelmingly male membership. This same attitude drove labor leaders to support new immigration restrictions that were passed during the 1900s and 1910s.

Government Steps In

Progressive efforts to curb corporate exploitation of workers were driven by the widespread perception that the robber barons—not lawmakers or the people they represented—had become the main architects of American society. The primary weapon that Progressives used against corporations was a sweeping new slate of governmental regulations. These regulations helped municipal, state, and local governments govern corporate behavior. But they were not imposed without a fight from the powerful corporations that had called the shots in America for so many years.

Reformers recognized that these companies were formidable foes. Corporations benefited from cheap labor, territorial expansion, new energy resources, and an almost complete absence of laws governing business behavior. Companies and trusts grew into economic Goliaths during the industrial revolution. By the Gilded Age, the use of mergers and unfriendly acquisitions of competitors to create mighty corporate giants had reached astounding levels. Between 1897 and 1904 alone, 4,227 firms merged to form 257 corporations. The largest of these mergers was the 1901 creation of the U.S. Steel Corporation. This new corporate giant, organized by financier J.P. Morgan, was worth an amazing

$1.4 billion and controlled 80 percent of the nation's steel production on the day of its creation.[39] By 1904 over 40 percent of the nation's total manufacturing output was controlled by 318 companies, and a single corporation produced over half the output in seventy-eight separate industries.[40]

At the dawn of the twentieth century, government had little legal power to slow the growing concentration of wealth and economic power in the hands of these mighty corporate machines. Corporations were very accomplished at using their influence to destroy proposed business regulations before state legislatures or Congress could pass them. And when reformers did manage to pass laws restricting corporate monopolies or reg-

Robert M. La Follette and the Progressive Ideal

Robert M. La Follette (1855–1925) served the people of Wisconsin in public office for most of his adult life. As governor of Wisconsin from 1901 to 1906, he pushed through many important business and political reforms. Thanks to La Follette's grit and statesmanship, Wisconsin became a model of state government for Progressives in other states. La Follette then moved on to Washington, D.C., where he served as a U.S. senator from 1906 until his death. During this period, he became known as perhaps the Senate's single greatest champion of Progressive causes. In the following excerpt from his 1913 autobiography, La Follette explained what motivated him to pursue Progressive ideals throughout his career:

If it can be shown that Wisconsin is a happier and better state to live in, that its institutions are more democratic, that the opportunities of all its people are more equal, that social justice more nearly prevails, that human life is safer and sweeter—then I shall rest content in the feeling that the Progressive movement has been successful. And I believe all these things can really be shown, and that there is no reason now why the movement should not expand until it covers the entire nation. While much has been accomplished, there is still a world of problems yet to be solved; we have just begun; there is hard fighting, and a chance for the highest patriotism, still ahead of us. The fundamental problem as to which shall rule, men or property, is still unsettled; it will require the highest qualities of heroism, the profoundest devotion to duty in this and in the coming generation, to reconstruct our institutions to meet the requirements of a new age. May such brave and true leaders develop that the people will not be led astray.

Source: Robert M. La Follette, *La Follette's Autobiography: A Personal Narrative of Political Experiences* (1913). Madison: University of Wisconsin Press, 1960.

ulating corporate activities, the business-friendly U.S. courts often ripped the laws to shreds or rendered them useless.

Business Reformers Fight the Courts

Many reformist efforts were actually blunted or turned aside by a U.S. court system that remained firmly on the side of corporations in matters of law. Many judges believed in a laissez-faire economic philosophy. According to this philosophy, government had no right to interfere with private business activity. Instead, it should let the free market operate without restrictions that would eventually smother economic growth and ultimately victimize all members of society. "Drawn mostly from the upper class, justices naturally defended the interests of property against labor," explained one scholar. "Moreover, courts rightly saw working-class mutualism [cooperative association] as a threat to their authority and to the individualist values embedded in the American common law."[41]

This attitude extended all the way to the U.S. Supreme Court. In the landmark 1905 case *Lochner v. New York*, for example, the justices struck down by a 5-4 vote a New York State law that limited the number of hours that bakery employees could work. "Statutes of the nature of that under review," declares the majority opinion, "limiting the hours in which grown and intelligent men may labor to earn their living are mere meddlesome interferences with the rights of the individual."[42]

This ruling, which ignored the pressure that bakery workers faced to work long hours or risk being fired, ushered in the so-called "Lochner era" in American legal history. During this era, which extended into the mid-1930s, the U.S. Supreme Court struck down or limited a number of Progressive government regulations that had been created to give new economic and workplace protections to American workers. In most cases, the Court stated that these new laws and regulations were unconstitutional.

Outrages and Triumphs

Faced with such clear hostility to their efforts, some reformers wondered if they would ever be successful in their efforts to rein in the nation's corporate giants. Over time, though, Progressives who were intent on imposing meaningful corporate reforms and improving the lives of workers fought through the setbacks and made steady progress. Ironically, infamous tragedies of American business history such as the Triangle Shirtwaist Factory Fire of 1911 and the 1914 Ludlow Massacre were important milestones in this campaign.

The Triangle Shirtwaist fire occurred on March 25, 1911, at a textile sweatshop in New York City. By the time the flames had been extinguished, 146 young immigrant women trapped in the inferno by locked exits and unsafe hallways had died.

The Ludlow Massacre occurred three years later, on April 20, 1914. In this incident, state militia under the direction of the Colorado Fuel and Iron Company—part of John D. Rockefeller Jr.'s

The 1911 Triangle Shirtwaist fire spurred the creation of important new safety reforms for New York factories.

were killed by militia. Afterward, the famous labor organizer Mary "Mother" Jones declared, "What does all this strife and turmoil growing out of the coal strike and the Ludlow Massacre mean? It means that the workers would rather die fighting to protect their women and children than to die in death-trap mines producing more wealth for the Rockefellers to use in crushing their children. . . . It means that the whole nation is on the verge of a revolution."[43]

To many union members and other working-class Americans, these events showed just how helpless they were in the face of corporate ruthlessness. But tragedies like the Triangle fire and the deaths in Ludlow actually generated important public and political support for meaningful business reforms and the wider Progressive cause. In the wake of the Triangle deaths, for example, the state of New York passed sweeping new fire safety regulations for factories and

corporate empire—attacked striking miners. The violence lasted for fourteen hours, during which time two women and eleven children in the miners' camp

established a factory investigation commission. Over the next several years, this commission recommended dozens of new workplace safety laws that were passed by lawmakers and completely transformed working conditions for thousands of employees across the state.

The events in Ludlow, meanwhile, prompted the creation of a federal commission on industrial relations to study labor-management strikes across America. The commission's final report endorsed many reforms sought by the nation's labor movement, including proposals to establish a national eight-hour work day and ban child labor.

The ever-strengthening public support for Progressive reform was the single most important factor in finally breaking down the walls the trusts had erected to preserve their empires. This support,

nurtured by muckraking journalists and eloquent activists—and heightened by events like the Triangle Shirtwaist tragedy—became particularly strong in middle-class communities that election-minded legislators could not ignore.

Another important factor in taking power back from America's corporations was the growing presence of Progressive-minded politicians in public office. In the 1890s and early 1900s, Progressives became mayors, state legislators, and U.S. congressmen in greater numbers than ever before. Reformers like Hazen S. Pingree (mayor of Detroit, 1890–1896), Tom Johnson (mayor of Cleveland, 1901–1909), Albert B. Cummins (governor and U.S.

The Ludlow Massacre of 1914 resulted in the death of two women and eleven children at a Colorado mining camp.

Roosevelt Condemns Corporate Influence in Politics

In 1910 former president Theodore Roosevelt delivered what became known as his "New Nationalism" speech. This speech summarized many of Roosevelt's Progressive political beliefs—and it turned out to be an early sign that Roosevelt was planning to run for president in 1912 (he eventually lost to Woodrow Wilson). Following is an excerpt from Roosevelt's speech about the continued "sinister influence" of corporations on American life and politics:

I stand for the square deal. But when I say that I am for the square deal, I mean not merely that I stand for fair play under the present rules of the game, but that I stand for having those rules changed so as to work for a more substantial equality of opportunity and of reward for equally good service. . . .

Now, this means that our government, National and State, must be freed from the sinister influence or control of special interests. Exactly as the special interests of cotton and slavery threatened our political integrity before the Civil War, so now the great special business interests too often control and corrupt the men and methods of government for their own profit. We must drive the special interests out of politics. . . . For every special interest is entitled to justice, but not one is entitled to a vote in Congress, to a voice on the bench, or to representation in any public office. The Constitution guarantees protection to property, and we must make that promise good. But it does not give the right of suffrage to any corporation.

Source: Theodore Roosevelt, *Theodore Roosevelt: An American Mind*, ed. Mario R. DiNunzio. New York: Penguin, 1995, p. 121.

Theodore Roosevelt was a strong opponent of political corruption.

senator for Iowa, 1902–1926), Robert M. La Follette (governor and U.S. senator for Wisconsin, 1901–1925), and Theodore Roosevelt (governor of New York, 1899–1900) effectively championed Progressive solutions to the wide variety of social, political, and economic problems troubling the nation. The biggest political event, though, was the inauguration of Roosevelt as the twenty-sixth president of the United States on September 14, 1901. When Roosevelt became president, a bold new age of corporate reform and government regulation began in America.

Chapter Four

U.S. Presidents of the Progressive Era

By the close of the nineteenth century, the desire to see fundamental changes made to American society, business, and politics had reached the boiling point in numerous farming communities, middle-class neighborhoods, and factories. But it was not until Theodore Roosevelt was sworn in as president of the United States in September 1901 that major Progressive reforms became a possibility.

When Roosevelt took office, the gathering forces of reform finally had the powerful ally they needed in the White House. Roosevelt shared their desire to reduce corporate dominance over the nation's affairs. He also shared the Progressive belief that government had a responsibility to battle the forces of poverty, greed, and injustice in American society. Finally, Roosevelt possessed the ambition and supreme self-confidence necessary to pursue those goals, no matter what obstacles were placed in his way. Bold and decisive, Roosevelt carried out a Progressive legislative agenda that changed the lives of millions of Americans. In the process, he became the single individual most closely identified with the entire Progressive Era.

From Frail Youth to Charismatic President

Roosevelt was born in New York City on October 27, 1858, to a prosperous merchant family. He was a small and sickly child, and his parents worried that he was destined for a short life. But even at a young age, Roosevelt displayed a high level of grit and determination. He took up boxing and weightlifting to improve his health and spent countless hours hunting, camping, and otherwise exploring the outdoors. By the time he graduated from Harvard University in 1880 he was a tough, hardy young man.

Roosevelt's career in politics began modestly with a two-year stint as a New

Theodore Roosevelt, center, and his band of "Rough Riders" during the Spanish American War of 1898.

Even at this early stage in his life, Roosevelt showed a strong Progressive streak. On July 4, 1886, for example, he electrified an audience of western farmers and ranchers with an Independence Day speech that blended patriotic pride with unmistakable hostility toward the greed of the nation's corporate robber barons. "Like all Americans, I like big things," he declared:

> Big prairies, big forests and mountains, big wheat fields, railroads—and herds of cattle too—big factories and steamboats and everything else. But we must keep steadily in mind that no people were ever yet benefited by riches if their prosperity corrupted their virtue. It is more important that we should show ourselves honest, brave, truthful, and intelligent than that we should own all the railways and grain elevators in the world. We have fallen heirs to the most glorious heritage a people ever received and each of us must do his part if we wish to show that this nation is worthy of its good fortune.[44]

In 1889 Roosevelt returned east to accept an appointment as a member of the U.S. Civil Service Commission. Over the next six years the reform-minded Repub-

York state assemblyman (1882–1884). In February 1884, though, his wife of four years, Alice Hathaway Lee Roosevelt, died after giving birth to their daughter Alice. The grieving Roosevelt fled to the Dakota Territory, where he worked as a cattle rancher and sheriff. Within a matter of a few years he was known throughout the territory for his larger-than-life personality and his fierce brand of patriotism. In 1886 he married Edith Kermit Carow, with whom he eventually had four sons and one daughter.

lican became known for his crusades against political corruption in New York City, and in 1895 he was appointed the city's police commissioner. He battled corrupt elements in the police force and further burnished his reputation as a principled public official by enforcing unpopular laws banning the sale of alcohol on Sundays. "I do not deal with public sentiment," he declared. "I deal with the law."[45]

In 1897 Roosevelt moved on to the position of assistant secretary of the navy. In May 1898 he resigned to fight in the Spanish American War. His exploits as colonel of the First U.S. Volunteer Cavalry Regiment—popularly known as Roosevelt's "Rough Riders"—made him a military hero by the time he returned to the United States several months later. Roosevelt then capitalized on his fame and his popularity with reformers across the state to win the governorship of New York on November 8, 1898. He served as governor for only two years, but during that time he passed state laws against child labor, abusive treatment of workers, and other causes dear to the hearts of American Progressives.

In 1900 Roosevelt was asked to run for vice president on the ticket of President William McKinley (McKinley's previous vice president, Garret Hobart, had died in office in November 1899). Roosevelt accepted the offer, and he spent the fall delivering spirited campaign speeches all across the country. The McKinley-Roosevelt ticket won the November 1900 presidential election by a comfortable margin over the Democratic ticket of William Jennings Bryan and Adlai E. Stevenson. Ten months later, though, McKinley was assassinated by a gunman in Buffalo, New York. He died on September 13, 1901, three days after the attack. Roosevelt was sworn in as America's twenty-sixth president one day later.

Progressive in the White House

When Roosevelt assumed the presidency, he became the youngest president in the nation's history. But despite his relative youth—and the fact that he had reached the Oval Office as a result of an assassin's bullet rather than the voters' ballot—Roosevelt governed from the outset with his trademark blend of ferocious determination, vigorous energy, and unshakable self-confidence.

Roosevelt also quickly served notice that he did not feel any obligation to blindly follow the pro-business policies of McKinley or the larger Republican Party. Only four months after being sworn in, Roosevelt delivered a rousing speech to Congress. He informed his listeners that he intended to tame the corporate trusts that dominated turn-of-the-century America. "The captains of industry who have driven the railway systems across this continent, who have built up our commerce, who have developed our manufactures, have on the whole done great good to our people," he acknowledged. "Without them the material development of which we are so justly proud could never have taken place. . . . Yet it is also true that there are

In 1902, only months after assuming the presidency, Theodore Roosevelt clashed with J.P. Morgan, one of the most powerful businessmen in America.

real and great evils [in corporate America] . . . and a resolute and practical effort must be made to correct these evils.[46]

Roosevelt's first big battles against the nation's corporate powers came the following year. In early 1902 the powerful financier J.P. Morgan maneuvered to combine two railroad lines into the Northern Securities Company. This merger would have given Morgan and his business allies a profitable stranglehold over rail transport between Chicago and the West Coast. When Roosevelt heard about the scheme, though, he used the antitrust restrictions of the almost forgotten Sherman Act to block it. Stunned by this development, Morgan frantically lobbied Roosevelt to let the deal go through. Roosevelt flatly refused on the grounds that the deal would give Morgan and his partners an unfair business monopoly. Morgan responded by unleashing his corporate attorneys on the administration, but in 1904 the Supreme Court sided with Roosevelt.

Several weeks later Roosevelt became engaged in an even more famous fight with powerful corporate interests. In May 1902 more than 147,000 members of the United Mine Workers (UMW) called

Roosevelt and the Muckrakers

Although he was a champion of many Progressive reforms, President Theodore Roosevelt disliked Upton Sinclair and many other crusading journalists of the era. He thought that they painted too grim a picture of American business and society, and he complained that their reports increased public support for radical and irresponsible "solutions" to America's ills.

In an April 15, 1906, speech, Roosevelt coined the term "muckraker" to describe these journalists. Today, the term is used to describe brave reporters who defy powerful interests. But when Roosevelt used the term, he was referring to a character in John Bunyan's novel Pilgrim's Progress *who never lifted his eyes from evil to admire the good in the world:*

Now it is very necessary that we should not flinch from seeing what is vile and debasing. There is filth on the floor, and it must be scraped up with the muck-rake: and there are times and places where this service is the most needed of all the services that can be performed. But the man who never does anything else, who never thinks or speaks or writes save of his feats with the muck-rake, speedily becomes, not a help to society, not an incitement to good, but one of the most potent forces for evil. . . .

If the whole picture is painted black there remains no hue whereby to single out the rascals for distinction from their fellows. Such painting finally induces a kind of moral color-blindness; and people affected by it come to the conclusion that no man is really black, and no man is really white, but they are all gray. . . . It becomes wellnigh hopeless to stir them either to wrath against wrong-doing or to enthusiasm for what is right; and such a mental attitude in the public gives hope to every knave, and is the despair of honest men.

Source: Theodore Roosevelt, "The Man with the Muck-Rake," *Putnam's Monthly and the Critic* 1, October 1906, pp. 42–43.

a strike against mine owners in Pennsylvania, home of the nation's largest anthracite coal mines. Weary of toiling exhausting hours in dangerous mines for paltry wages, the strikers demanded corporate recognition of the UMW, higher pay, and other concessions. The mine owners responded with contempt, refusing all requests to even meet with UMW representatives.

Roosevelt monitored the situation quietly for several months, but the prospect of winter coal shortages eventually roused him to action. In October he organized and supervised a conference between UMW president John Mitchell and the mine owners. The haughty attitude of the mine owners angered Roosevelt so much that he announced that he was thinking about using federal troops to seize the mines and operate them until the mine owners agreed to arbitration to settle the strike. This stunning threat convinced management to agree to arbitration. A few months later the arbitration panel granted the miners a wage increase and agreed to several other union demands. Even more important, Roosevelt's stand with the miners had great symbolic value. "The federal government, for the first time in its history, had intervened in a strike not to break it, but to bring about a peaceful settlement. The great anthracite strike of 1902 cast a long shadow."[47]

Roosevelt's "Square Deal"

As Roosevelt's 1904 reelection campaign approached, he seemed assured of remaining in the White House. For one thing, most Americans enjoyed his vigorous, confident personality. As author Edith Wharton commented, "He was so alive at all points, and so gifted with the rare faculty of living intensely and entirely in every moment as it passed, that each [encounter with Roosevelt] glows in me like a tiny morsel of radium."[48]

Americans also respected Roosevelt's exploits as a hunter and soldier, and they admired his great and restless intellect. As one biographer wrote,

"[Roosevelt] is capable of declaiming German poetry to Lutheran preachers, and comparing recently resuscitated Gaelic letters with Hopi Indian lyrics. He is recognized as the world authority on big American game mammals. . . . Roosevelt is equally at home with experts in naval strategy, forestry, Greek drama, cowpunching metaphysics, protective coloration, and football techniques.[49]

Finally, Roosevelt had the all-important support of the American middle-class, which had become firmly Progressive in its outlook in the opening years of the twentieth century. "Progressives believed that government at every level—local, state, and federal—had to be enrolled in the fight [for fairness and democracy] through the direct participation of the people," said one historian. "Legislation was necessary to protect woman and child workers, to clean up slums, improve housing, and control the great corporations, but first government itself had to be

Roosevelt met with labor leaders and mine owners in 1902 in order to settle the Pennsylvania coal mine strike.

reformed. And to do that it was necessary to rescue the democratic process from interest groups whose only concern was in increasing their power and profits."[50] During Roosevelt's first three years in office, Progressive-minded Americans had become convinced that he was the right man to tackle such reforms.

Roosevelt emphasized his reputation as a bold reformer throughout the 1904 election campaign. He promised a Square Deal administration in which no interest group would receive preferential treatment over another. His words triggered grumbling from pro-business Republicans who disliked Roosevelt's trust-busting policies. But they stayed quiet because they feared the prospect of a populist Democratic administration even more.

As predicted, Roosevelt cruised to re-election, winning about 57 percent of the popular vote against Democratic nominee Alton B. Parker (38 percent) and Socialist candidate Eugene Debs (3 percent). Roosevelt accurately interpreted the election results as a mandate for his Progressive policies, and he spent the next four years in the White House pushing one bold initiative after another.

A Moderate Maverick

During his second term in office, Roosevelt prosecuted more than 40 antitrust cases against corporate giants, pushed the United States into a much more prominent role in international affairs, and changed government's role in American society in many important ways. But despite all this, most of Roosevelt's Progressive ideals and policies did not stray into radical territory. He was at heart a political moderate who firmly supported ethical businesses and industries that expanded the American economy and benefited ordinary consumers. In fact, one of his chief motivations in challenging powerful corporations, battling political corruption, and addressing social problems was to keep more radical forces in American society from gaining influence.

This political cartoon shows Theodore Roosevelt controlling a bucking bronco, which represents the large corporate trusts that, prior to Roosevelt, had taken over the American economy.

BRONCO BUSTING IN THE WEST
"Amuses us and don't hurt the hoss"

During his last years in the White House, Roosevelt openly complained about some of the Progressive activists and journalists who railed against political and corporate corruption. He believed that some of the most prominent reformers were fools who were not respected by working-class Americans. "[They lack the] slightest understanding of the needs, interests, ways of thought, and convictions of the average small man,"[51] he charged.

Roosevelt also believed that an ugly undertone of envy was present in some criticisms of the wealthy and powerful. "The unscrupulous rich man who seeks to exploit and oppress those who are less well off is in spirit not opposed to, but identical with, the unscrupulous poor man who desires to plunder and oppress those who are better off,"[52] he once said. On another occasion he freely acknowledged that "we are passing through a period of great unrest—social, political, and industrial unrest." But he went on to warn that

> so far as this movement of agitation throughout the country takes the form of a fierce discontent with evil, of a determination to punish the authors of evil, whether in industry or politics, the feeling is to be heartily welcomed as a sign of healthy life. If, on the other hand, it turns into a mere crusade of appetite against appetite, of a contest between the brutal greed of the "have-nots" and the brutal greed of the "haves," then it has no significance for good, but only for evil.[53]

Bold Initiatives and Sweeping Acts

These concerns, however, did not prevent Roosevelt from overhauling the guiding philosophy of American government during his second term in office. He believed that the role of government in American society had to be expanded in order for the nation to absorb the huge cultural and economic changes brought about by the industrial revolution. He was convinced that the future of the republic hinged on restoring public faith in the basic principles of justice and democracy upon which the United States had been founded.

This belief drove Roosevelt's decision to support a wide range of new business regulations during his second term. He persuaded Congress to create a bureau of corporations to investigate and regulate big business. He also used his self-described "bully pulpit"—the Oval Office—to generate widespread public support for numerous laws designed to improve workplace safety, stop child labor, punish slumlords, weed out political corruption, and help small business owners.

One of Roosevelt's greatest triumphs was the strengthening of the Interstate Commerce Commission (ICC). When he signed the Hepburn Act in 1906, the law empowered the ICC to set reasonable railroad rates for passenger travel and shipping and prosecute companies that engaged in unethical business practices. The Hepburn Act also forced the previously all-powerful railroad companies to sell off business interests in mining,

Theodore Roosevelt, standing in Yellowstone National Park, believed strongly in preserving America's natural resources for future generations.

steam shipping, and many other industries.

Roosevelt also defied powerful corporate interests by protecting immense tracts of American wilderness from exploitative logging, mining, and other development. During its first 125 years of existence, the United States had set aside very little of its land for conservation. To the contrary, territorial, state, and federal government had let corporations plunder the nation's forests, rivers, and mineral resources for generations. Roosevelt set a dramatic new course in America's treatment of its abundant—but not inexhaustible—natural resources.

By the time Roosevelt left the White House in 1909, he had founded 51 wildlife refuges, established 18 national monuments, created 5 new national parks, and added almost 50 million acres (20 million ha) to the nation's previously threadbare forest system. Some of these areas, such as national forests, continued to be utilized commercially. But the Roosevelt administration passed laws and established agencies to ensure that these resources would be used more responsibly—and thus to ensure that the country's natural resources would be passed along intact to future generations. Roosevelt, wrote one biographer, "was able to merge his love of nature and its beauty with his protective instincts, to offer [his conservation program] as a gift to all Americans in perpetuity. Little or, perhaps, nothing else gave him more satisfaction as a public servant."[54]

By the time Roosevelt left the presidency on March 3, 1909, he had changed the way Americans thought about the role of government in their lives. He had also given the Progressive movement many of its greatest triumphs. His successors—first William Howard Taft and then Woodrow Wilson—would build on his record of progressivism. But neither man would capture the hearts of Progressives in the way that Theodore Roosevelt did during his years in the White House.

Corporate Reform under Taft and Wilson

Many business regulations became a reality during the administrations of presidents William Howard Taft (who served from 1909 to 1913) and Woodrow Wilson (1913–1921). Both Taft and Wilson recognized the continued public demand for increased government oversight of corporate behavior and economic activity, and many of their business policies reflected this reformist spirit. "We have come upon a very different age from any that preceded us," agreed Woodrow Wilson during a 1912 campaign stop.

There is a sense in which in our day the individual has been submerged. In most parts of the country men work, not for themselves, not as partners in the old way in which they used to work, but generally as employees—in a higher or lower grade—of great corporations. There was a time when corporations played a very minor part in our business affairs, but now they play the chief part, and most men are the servants of the corporations.[55]

The Taft administration enjoyed several major victories in its efforts to restore greater balance to the relationship between American corporations and their employees and customers. Taft supported the Mann-Elkins Act of 1910, an important law that brought the nation's powerful telephone, telegraph, and cable industries under increased government regulation. He also carried on Roosevelt's legacy of trust-busting. His administration broke up numerous corporate trusts, including Standard Oil, which was the largest company in American history until its dissolution in 1911.

Taft also pushed two important pieces of antitrust legislation that eventually became law during Wilson's presidency. The first of these, the Federal Trade Commission Act, was passed in September 1914. It established the Federal Trade Commission (FTC) and gave it powers to eliminate and prevent business monopolies in all industries. The FTC also was given authority to ensure fair business competition among corporations of all shapes and sizes.

The second of these acts, the Clayton Antitrust Act of 1914, was signed into law by Wilson in October. This legislation was essentially a much tougher version of the 1890 Sherman Antitrust Act. It outlawed mergers and a variety of unfair business practices, including exclusive sales contracts, local price-cutting designed to bankrupt smaller competitors, and rebates. The Clayton Act also formally legalized peaceful labor actions like strikes, boycotts, and picketing, and it placed the nation's first restrictions on judges' use of injunctions against labor activity.

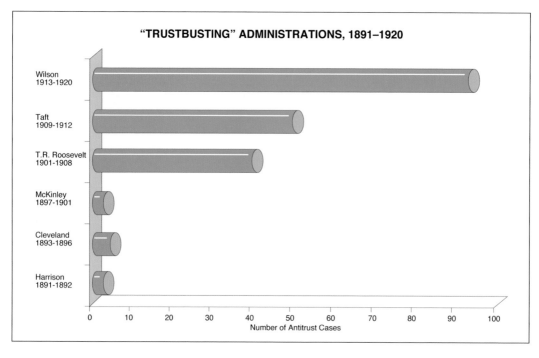

"TRUSTBUSTING" ADMINISTRATIONS, 1891–1920

Wilson
1913-1920

Taft
1909-1912

T.R. Roosevelt
1901-1908

McKinley
1897-1901

Cleveland
1893-1896

Harrison
1891-1892

Number of Antitrust Cases

The Schoolmaster of Politics

Woodrow Wilson, who served as the twenty-eighth president of the United States from March 1913 to March 1921, was born on December 28, 1856, in Staunton, Virginia. The son of a Presbyterian minister, he grew up in the South. As a young adult he moved north and carved out a successful career as college teacher and administrator. But he always regarded himself as a Southerner, and he carried that region's strong racial prejudices with him for the rest of his life.

In 1902 Wilson was named president of Princeton University in New Jersey. He served in that position for eight years. In 1910 he won the governorship of New Jersey as a Democrat. During this period, Wilson's aloof manner and his past career in higher education prompted newspapers to call him the "schoolmaster of politics." But his Progressive ideals made him popular with the state's citizenry, and Democratic Party leaders became convinced that he was an attractive presidential candidate.

Wilson won the party's presidential nomination in 1912 and cruised to election, in large part because Republicans split their vote between Republican candidate William Taft and former president Theodore Roosevelt, who waged an independent campaign. Wilson also easily won reelection in 1916. During Wilson's two terms, he advanced the

Progressive agenda in many areas and successfully guided the nation through World War I. After the war, however, his efforts to create an international League of Nations proved unpopular with many Americans. He also retreated from Progressive policies in the face of mounting public resistance.

After leaving the White House in March 1921, Wilson's health rapidly declined. He died on February 3, 1924, at his home in Washington, D.C.

Source: H.W. Brands, *Woodrow Wilson*. New York: Times Books, 2003.

President Woodrow Wilson.

Welfare Capitalism

As the Progressive movement gained strength in America during the end of the nineteenth century and the first two decades of the twentieth century, many large companies turned to welfare capitalism. Under these plans, companies invested large sums of money in social and education programs for their employees. Industrial giants such as U.S. Steel, General Electric, Ford Motor Company, International Harvester, National Cash Register, and H.J. Heinz paid for company baseball teams, gardening clubs, marching bands, swimming pools, nursing clinics, cooking classes, citizenship classes, and other perks. Some companies even offered profit sharing and private pension plans for employees who qualified (usually a small percentage of the overall work force).

Management typically characterized these programs as examples of their respect and appreciation for their employees. Union leaders and business reformers did not view these programs in the same way. They charged that welfare capitalism was nothing more than bribery intended to keep employees from supporting or joining unions. According to these critics, corporations had figured out that it was cheaper for them to pay for baseball uniforms, gardens, and sewing classes than it was for them to agree to wage hikes or shorter work weeks.

Source: Andrea Tone, *The Business of Benevolence: Industrial Paternalism in Progressive America*. Ithaca, NY: Cornell University Press, 1997.

By the time America entered World War I in 1918, these acts—combined with a host of more narrowly targeted laws such as the 1916 Adamson Act (which mandated an eight-hour workday for railroad employees) and the 1915 La Follette Seamen's Act (which dramatically increased the legal rights of American sailors employed by private companies)—had ushered in a new age of government regulation over the affairs of business and commerce.

Chapter Five

The End of the Progressive Era

By the mid-1910s the Progressive Era was in full swing. Government regulation of corporate behavior had jumped dramatically, and all sorts of reform organizations and government agencies had been created to address the nation's social problems. Only a few short years later, though, the Age of Reform was over. Why did the Progressive movement crash in such spectacular fashion? More than any other reason, it fell apart because World War I and other international events prompted a strong public and corporate backlash against government regulations that came to be viewed as incompatible with American principles of freedom and individuality.

America's Entrance into the Great War

The United States was not the only country that had been dramatically changed by the industrial revolution. The nations of Europe had also experienced great economic growth and social turmoil. By the early twentieth century the continent had become an explosive cauldron of social upheaval, shifting military alliances, and ambition for greater wealth and power.

The event that ignited all of these volatile elements was the assassination of Archduke Franz Ferdinand of Austria on June 28, 1914. He was killed by a fanatic from neighboring Serbia, a country with which Austria had tense relations. Austria's desire to punish Serbia for this shocking murder was supported by Germany, which was ruled by an ambitious military government that had amassed the largest army in the world. But Russia, France, and Great Britain all had military treaties with Serbia, so they rushed to the country's defense.

During the next few weeks, political leaders in Europe showed little interest in avoiding war. Instead, patriotic pride, the desire to seize new territory and power, and longstanding prejudices against other nationalities drove all these nations to mobilize their armies against one another. By August, Europe had divided into two camps—the Allies (led by Russia, France, and Britain) and the Central Powers (spearheaded by Germany, Turkey, and Austria-Hungary)—and entered into World War I, also known as "the Great War."

For the next three years the warring armies attacked each other—and the cities of Europe—with brutal force. The conflict marked the first widespread use of chemical weapons, the first mass bombardment of civilians by airplane, and the first genocide of the twentieth century (when more than one million ethnic Armenians perished at the hands of Turkey's racist government). By war's end, more than 8.5 million soldiers and as many as 10 million civilians had been killed.

The Great War was a virtual stalemate until 1917, when the United States entered the conflict on the side of the Allies. President Woodrow Wilson, who described America's entrance into the war as a quest "to make the world safe for democracy," retooled the nation's government and its massive industrial resources for the war effort. By early 1918 it was clear that the economic, industrial, and military strength of the United States had swung the balance of power decisively toward the Allies. With each passing month, the military position of Germany and the other Central Powers became more precarious. One by one, Germany's allies gave up the fight, and on November 11, 1918, Germany signed an armistice with the Allies that basically amounted to an unconditional surrender.

Progressivism During the Great War

Progressive leaders in America had splintered over the issue of entering World War I. Supporters of the idea, such as Social Gospel leader Lyman Abbott and journalist Walter Lippman, argued that by joining the fight against the authoritarian regime in Germany, Americans would be further inspired to support Progressive reforms at home. "We shall turn with fresh interest to our own tyrannies—to our Colorado mines, our autocratic steel industries, our sweatshops and our slums,"[56] predicted Lippman.

Other Progressive leaders condemned America's entrance into the war, however. Some critics, such as Jane Addams, opposed this decision because of their pacifist beliefs. They formed an important part of a vocal peace movement within America during this time. Others feared that the war would restore too much power to American industry, which would be responsible for supplying the U.S. military with airplanes, ships, ammunition, uniforms, and countless other supplies. Many of these same skeptics also worried that the war effort would distract America from its domestic problems.

Initially, it appeared that these fears would not come to pass. In fact, some historians regard the months of American involvement in World War I as the pinnacle of the Progressive Era.

As American soldiers fought overseas to make the world safe for

*The warship USS **Arizona** was launched in early 1917, just as the United States was preparing to enter World War I.*

Once the United States entered World War I, large corporations—once viewed as the enemy of working-class Americans—became valued for their ability to quickly churn out war materials.

democracy, the administration of Woodrow Wilson worked feverishly to create a wartime model for a peacetime Progressive utopia. Against the backdrop of wartime struggle and sacrifice, reformers managed to outlaw alcohol, close down vice districts, win suffrage for women, expand the income tax, and take over the railroads.[57]

By the time that America emerged victorious from the Great War, however, the American public had decided that the federal government now exerted *too much* control over the American economy and society. The backlash quickly became so loud and sustained that even Wilson was forced to acknowledge it and change his approach to governing. "Rather than an advertisement for a progressive future," wrote one scholar, "the Wilsonian war effort became the death knell for the progressive movement."[58]

Disillusionment and Anger

Several factors drove Americans away from the Progressive ideas that had dominated the nation's politics for nearly two decades. Economic anxiety was one big issue. The cost of paying for the war led the Wilson administration to raise taxes on the middle class, which in turn set off a wave of inflation that frightened poor, working-class, and middle-class Americans.

Another issue was the war's role in changing public perceptions about American business. For decades, large segments of the American population had seen the nation's corporations as ruthless giants that crushed everything in their path. Similarly, they regarded the country's leading industrialists as cold-hearted robber barons with an unquenchable thirst for money. But after the United States entered World War I, government agencies, newspapers, magazines, and corporate spokesmen alike praised the role of American industry in outfitting the nation's armed forces. The war made many people realize that whatever their shortcomings, America's factories, railroads, and banks also were a tremendous national asset.

The Wilson administration made several decisions to restrict basic constitutional freedoms during the war. This led many citizens to conclude that government oversight of American society was reaching unhealthy levels. The administration's decision to impose a draft to fill up the military ranks was enormously unpopular in many parts of the country. The Justice Department also authorized the 200,000 members of a pro-war volunteer group called the American Protective League to report on suspected spies and "slackers"[59] who failed to buy war bonds or show sufficient enthusiasm for the war.

In addition, the government passed a number of sweeping war measures designed to silence or imprison anyone who obstructed the war effort. These laws included the Alien Act, the Alien Enemies Act, the Espionage Act, the Sedition Act, and the Trading with the Enemy Act. Critics believed that by passing such laws, the Wilson administration was trampling on the same democratic ideals that it claimed to have gone to war to defend.

Many Americans caught up in the patriotic fervor of wartime dismissed these charges. Instead, they spent more of their energy working to support the war effort—or vilifying outspoken opponents of the war like anarchist Emma Goldman, Socialist Party leader Eugene Debs, and Bill Haywood, president of the radical Industrial Workers of the World (IWW). Even mainstream opponents of the war, like Addams, were condemned as anti-American. To many supporters of America's entrance into World War I, anyone who questioned the war was guilty of treason.

As the war went on, though, even steadfast supporters of the war voiced anger about the rising number of government-imposed restrictions on business practices and private behavior. According to this perspective, "every male between 18 and 45 had been deprived of freedom of his body," stated journalist and historian Mark Sullivan.

Every person had been deprived of freedom of his tongue. . . . Every business man was shorn of dominion over his factory or store, every housewife surrendered control of her table, every farmer was forbidden to sell his wheat except at the price the government fixed. . . . In America the state took back, the individual gave up, what had taken centuries of contest to win.[60]

Another important factor in the decline of progressivism was the death of Theodore Roosevelt in 1916, just a few months before the United States entered World War I. Roosevelt's passing deprived the Progressive movement of its most popular and eloquent champion. By the time America emerged from wartime in early 1919, Roosevelt's death seemed like a powerful omen that the Age of Reform had run its course.

Postwar America and the Russian Revolution

World War I had left many of the traditional European powers in terrible condition, but the United States emerged from the war with a roaring economy and a citizenry that was flush with the thrill of victory. Exhilarated and relieved Americans rushed to stores to buy the new consumer products being produced by the nation's corporations. These large companies had emerged from the war with enormous sums of money to invest in new factories, new machinery, and campaign contributions for politicians that they hoped to influence. Once the nation's soldiers returned home, Americans basked in the knowledge that their nation was the world's newest financial and military superpower.

But the end of the Great War also brought new uncertainties and challenges. During the war, African Americans from the South had flooded into northern cities to work in the factories and shipyards that operated day and night to provide American troops with ships, guns, uniforms, blankets, and other supplies. Once the war ended, however, white soldiers returned home

The Sedition Act of 1918

On May 16, 1918, the U.S. Congress passed the Sedition Act, which imposed jail sentences and heavy fines on any American who dared "utter, print, write, or publish any disloyal, profane, scurrilous, or abusive language about the form of government of the United States" while the nation was at war. This law, which was a blatant violation of the First Amendment of the U.S. Bill of Rights guaranteeing free speech, was used to silence a large number of pacifists and other critics of American involvement in World War I.

The most famous use of the Sedition Act came against Eugene V. Debs, the pacifist labor organizer who had run for president in 1900 as a Social Democrat and in 1904,

1908, and 1912 on the Socialist Party of America ticket. After Debs gave an antiwar speech in June 1918 in Canton, Ohio, he was arrested, tried and sentenced to ten years in prison under the Sedition Act. Debs appealed the decision, and the case eventually reached the U.S. Supreme Court, which upheld his conviction. Undaunted, Debs launched yet another presidential campaign from his prison cell in 1920. One year later, Congress repealed the Sedition Act and Debs's sentence was commuted.

Source: Melvyn Dubofsky and Foster Rhea Dulles, *Labor in America: A History*, 7th ed. Wheeling, IL: Harlan Davidson, 2004.

Labor leader Eugene V. Debs.

and the competition for jobs and housing intensified. African Americans almost always lost these struggles due to the rampant racism and discrimination of the era. Even so, incidents of white violence against blacks soared in many parts of the country.

The wartime demand for factory workers and other laborers also bolstered the ranks of many unions. The membership of the American Federation of Labor (AFL), for example, jumped from 2.6 million in 1916 to 65 million by 1920. The AFL and other growing unions held off on confronting management over work issues as long as America was at war.

After the conflict ended, though, the labor movement moved quickly to capture its share of the economic riches that flowed in postwar America. When corporate leaders rejected many of these demands, labor unrest exploded across the

"Big Bill" Haywood and the Wobblies

I n all of American labor history, few individuals were as loved and hated as "Big Bill" Haywood, the radical activist who led the Industrial Workers of the World for much of the Progressive Era. Born in Salt Lake City in 1869, Haywood was raised in poverty. By age nine he was working in underground mines, and he never received a formal education.

Haywood's life as a labor organizer began in the mid-1890s, when he became a leader of an Idaho chapter of the Western Federation of Miners. Within a few years he had emerged as a leading figure in the national union—and one of the most radical voices for labor rights in the American West. In 1905 Haywood helped found the Industrial Workers of the World, often known as the "Wobblies."

One year later Haywood was charged with plotting the assassination of former Idaho governor Frank Steunenberg. He was acquitted, though, and he returned to the IWW, where he courted controversy with his fiery condemnations of big business. In 1915 he became the formal head of the IWW. After the Russian Revolution of 1917, Haywood and other Wobblies expressed open support for Vladimir Lenin and his Communist regime. This support, combined with Haywood's condemnation of American involvement in World War I, made him a target of the federal government. In 1917 Haywood was arrested by authorities and charged with violating espionage and sedition acts. He was convicted but remained free on bail while his appeals were heard. When the Supreme Court rejected his appeal in 1921, Haywood fled to the Soviet Union, where he died in 1928.

Source: Peter Carlson, *Roughneck: The Life and Times of Big Bill Haywood*. New York: Norton, 1983.

country. In 1919 nearly one-fourth of the entire U.S. labor force participated in labor strikes against employers. Participants in these strikes ranged from Boston policemen to Seattle port workers to Pennsylvania steel workers.

Many of these strikes failed, in large measure because management succeeded in branding strikers as Bolshevik agents or sympathizers. The Bolsheviks were Communists who had in 1917 top-

pled the Russian dictator Czar Nicholas II and installed an authoritarian Communist government headed by Vladimir Lenin. In March 1918 the Communists signed a separate peace treaty with Germany—a move that was viewed as a terrible betrayal by the United States and Russia's other wartime allies.

The bloody Russian Revolution, which culminated in the execution of Nicholas II and his entire royal family, greatly alarmed the United States. The new Communist regime fiercely opposed private property, capitalism, and individual rights. Instead, Lenin and his Bolshevik supporters were dedicated to establishing a classless political system in which the state controlled all aspects of the economy and society. The Bolsheviks also voiced confidence that communism would soon sweep over the rest of the world.

The "Red Scare"

American fear and distrust of communism surged after the war, when many Americans began to associate Bolshevism with two controversial segments of the U.S. population—labor union members and immigrants. The American labor move-

ment and many of the nation's recent immigrants did hold liberal political beliefs. Their calls for social justice and condemnations of greedy corporate "capitalists" even echoed some of the language used by Lenin and other Communist leaders. In addition, some high-profile labor groups, such as the Industrial Workers of the World (IWW), proudly championed Socialist solutions to America's problems. Finally, many Americans remained angry about the antiwar positions that some labor leaders and immigrants had taken during World War I.

As fears that Communists, or Reds, were infiltrating America spread like wildlife, many immigrants and labor leaders tried to reassure the public of

Russian immigrants targeted as Communist radicals are chained together and taken to the emigration station in Boston, Massachusetts, for questioning.

their patriotism. They pointed out that fighting social injustice and corporate greed was not the same as advocating the overthrow of the American political system. They also noted that union members and immigrants, who fought as soldiers and manned the wartime assembly lines, had played an important role in defeating Germany in the Great War.

These efforts had little impact, though. Instead, the United States succumbed to fear and paranoia, and the notorious Red Scare of 1919–1920 swept across the land. During these months, immigrants and unions were targeted for raids, intimidation, and violence. In an effort to cripple unions and maximize corporate profits, many large companies effectively promoted the idea that labor organizations were strongholds of Bolshevism. When Midwestern steel workers launched a general strike in 1919, for example, company owners successfully portrayed the strikers—many of whom were immigrants—as dangerous radicals who threatened the American way of life. In one Pittsburgh newspaper, a steel company paid for an advertisement that was nominally aimed at strikers—but was also targeted at the larger public:

AMERICA IS CALLING YOU

This is no ordinary strike. Rather it must be looked upon as the diabolical attempt of a small group of radicals to disorganize labor and plant revolution in this country. . . . Keep America busy, and prosperous, and American. Go back to work.[61]

This corporate strategy worked time and time again. Striking workers seethed at the attacks on their patriotism, but their protests were drowned out by corporate propaganda and newspaper editorials that equated calls for better wages and working conditions with communism. "[One cannot be] a loyal American unless . . . you give up all the rights your country gives you and obey your employer,"[62] despaired one worker. Another union man complained that even though "your position may be perfectly in harmony with the fundamental law of the country, the industrial autocrat will shout you down. . . . So long as you have not the power to enforce your thoughts you are like one crying in the wilderness."[63]

Last Days of Progressivism

Labor unions and other victims of the Red Scare turned to the Wilson administration for help, but they were turned away. By this time, Wilson and many other American politicians had changed course with the shifting political winds. They did not want to be viewed as sympathetic to groups that were distrusted by so many American voters.

In addition, Wilson's attention was elsewhere. In 1919 he devoted nearly all of his energies to generating support in Washington for the newly founded League of Nations, an international body designed to use diplomacy to prevent future wars. In the fall of 1919, however, he suffered a stroke that limited his ability to campaign for the League. In the end, the U.S. Senate never ratified the treaty, and the United States never joined the League.

Even before his stroke, however, Wilson had distanced himself from the Progressive movement, which many Americans now linked with Bolshevik labor radicals and immigrant troublemakers. By 1920 most Americans seemed to want the Progressives who had spent the last few decades shining a light on the nation's social problems and economic inequities to just go away. "To question the wisdom of the powers that be, to advance new and disturbing ideas, had ceased to be an act of virtue, the proof of an aspiring spirit," wrote the famed Progressive lawyer Donald Richberg. "Such attitudes were 'radical' and 'destructive.' . . . Progressivism was losing its supreme asset—respectability."[64]

In November 1920 the U.S. presidential election decisively completed America's turn away from progressivism—even though it was the first national election since woman suffrage, one of the greatest triumphs of the Age of Reform. Democratic nominee James Cox and his running mate, future president Franklin D. Roosevelt, were trounced by the Republican ticket of Warren G. Harding and Calvin Coolidge. Harding and Coolidge were stout defenders of American business, and

During the "Red Scare" of 1919–1920, any literature that was deemed subversive in any way was immediately confiscated and destroyed.

they vowed to loosen governmental oversight of the American economy and restore stability to daily American life.

The Legacy of the Progressive Era

During the 1920s Progressive voices in America were in full retreat. Courts and legislatures alike worked to roll back regulations governing corporate behavior and laws meant to address poverty and other social problems. The so-called Roaring Twenties also saw American culture emphasize pleasure and merriment and personal freedom like never before. In this period of general middle-class prosperity, many Americans were not interested in hearing about the continued struggles of the poor or the ways in which corporate powers had regained their lost influence over the country's

policies on everything from international trade to natural resource conservation.

In 1929, however, the Great Depression rocked America and the world. This terrible economic downturn caused massive job losses across the United States and financially ruined millions of families. Confronted by this mortal threat to the nation, President Franklin D. Roosevelt (who was a fifth cousin to Theodore Roosevelt) responded with the New Deal following his inauguration in January 1933. This ambitious set of federal programs reflected Roosevelt's belief that the Great Depression could not be beaten without the active intervention of the national government.

During the ensuing six-year New Deal era, the Roosevelt administration passed new banking reform laws, funded work and agricultural relief programs, gave

As the Progressive Era faded in the early 1920s, it was replaced by the "Roaring Twenties," a time when many Americans were doing better economically and were able to spend their money as they pleased.

Herbert Croly and Modern Liberalism

The Progressive editor and author Herbert David Croly, who founded the influential magazine *New Republic* and wrote several highly respected books on American politics and culture, is sometimes described as the godfather of modern liberalism. Born on January 23, 1869, in New York City, Croly became a respected editor with a strong Progressive streak.

Croly did not achieve a national reputation, though, until the Progressive Era was in full swing. In 1909 he published *The Promise of American Life,* in which he explained his belief that a strong national government and individual rights could coexist in a democratic society. The book reportedly made a big impression on Theodore Roosevelt, the foremost Progressive politician of the age, as well as other Progressive activists. In 1914 he founded the *New Republic,* which quickly became the nation's best-known Progressive magazine. Croly remained the editor of the *New Republic* until his death on May 17, 1930. Today, Croly's works continue to be cited as enduring influences in modern American liberal political thought.

Source: Edward A. Stettner, *Shaping American Liberalism: Herbert Croly and Progressive Thought.* Lawrence: University of Kansas Press, 1993.

new protections to unions and other working Americans, established the Social Security pension system for elderly and disabled Americans, and introduced numerous other initiatives to help struggling Americans. In short, Roosevelt and the New Deal drew upon the example and spirit of the Progressive Era to defend the American people from the massive unemployment and economic turmoil of the Great Depression.

Since that time, the shadow of the Progressive Era has waxed and waned over the United States. "From 1960 to 1980, America experienced sharp swings between the progressive and conservative approaches," wrote one scholar. "But it also experienced periods of political stalemate when progressives and conservatives fought to a draw."[65] And despite these political swings, the federal government has remained an important part of daily American life for nearly a century.

This influence has been hotly debated over the years. Conservatives believe that excessive government authority has stifled personal liberties, eroded traditions of self-reliance and independence, and hampered economic growth that benefits all Americans. President Ronald Reagan famously summarized this viewpoint in 1981 when he declared that government was not the solution to America's problems, but rather that "government is the problem."[66]

During the Great Depression years of the 1930s, numerous government aid programs were established to help people earn a living. Here, a Farm Security Administration supervisor discusses a plan with a farmer to get his farm back working.

Progressive Americans profoundly disagree with this assessment. To the contrary, they feel that government involvement in the affairs of American society and business has helped—and continues to help—the nation grow and prosper. As Progressive historian Arthur J. Schlesinger wrote in 2001:

The record surely shows that the intervention of national authority . . . has given a majority of Americans more personal dignity and liberty than they ever had before. The individual freedoms destroyed have been in the main the freedom to deny black Americans their elementary rights as American citizens, the freedom to work little children in mills and immigrants in sweatshops, the freedom to pay starvation wages and enforce dawn-to-dusk working hours and permit squalid working conditions, the freedom to deceive in the sale of goods and securities and drugs, the freedom to loot national resources and pollute the environment, and so on. These are all freedoms, one supposes, that a civilized country can readily do without.[67]

Notes

Introduction: Industrialization Ushers in the Progressive Era

1. Michael McGerr, *A Fierce Discontent: The Rise and Fall of the Progressive Movement in America*. New York: Oxford University Press, 2005, pp. 4, 6.

Chapter One: The Age of Industrialization

2. Alex Groner and Editors of *Business Week* and *American Heritage, The American Heritage History of American Business and Industry*. New York: American Heritage, 1972, p. 11.
3. McGerr, *A Fierce Discontent*, p. 33.
4. McGerr, *A Fierce Discontent*, p. 8.
5. Andrew Carnegie, *The Gospel of Wealth and Other Timely Essays*, ed. Edward C. Kirkland (1900). Cambridge, MA: Belknap Press of Harvard University, 1962, p. 18.
6. Benjamin Harrison, *Views of an Ex-president*. Indianapolis: Bowen-Merrill, 1901, p. 336.
7. David Traxel, *Crusader Nation: The United States in Peace and the Great War 1898–1920*. New York: Alfred A. Knopf, 2006, p. 6.
8. McGerr, *A Fierce Discontent*, p. 12.
9. Frederick Jaher, "The Gilded Elite: American Multimillionaires, 1865 to the Present," in *Wealth and the Wealthy in the Modern World*, ed. W.D. Rubin-

stein. New York: Palgrave Macmillan, 1980, p. 200.
10. John Mitchell, "An Exposition and Interpretation of the Trade Union Movement," in *The Christian Ministry and the Social Order*, ed. Charles S. McFarland. New Haven, CT: Yale University Press, 1913, p. 90.
11. Traxel, *Crusader Nation*, p. 9.
12. William Allen White, *The Autobiography of William Allen White*. New York: Macmillan, 1946, p. 390.
13. Traxel, *Crusader Nation*, pp. 15–16.
14. Quoted in Clarence Darrow, *Verdicts out of Court*, eds. Arthur Weinberg and Lila Weinberg. Chicago: Elephant Paperbacks, 1989, p. 64.

Chapter Two: Social and Political Reforms of the Progressive Era

15. James N. Gregory, *The Southern Diaspora: How the Great Migrations of Black and White Southerners Transformed America*. Chapel Hill: University of North Carolina Press, 2007, p. 23.
16. Anthony Lukas, *Big Trouble*. New York: Simon & Schuster, 1997, p. 305.
17. Quoted in William Cronon, *Nature's Metropolis: Chicago and the Great West*. New York: Norton, 1991, p. 9.
18. Traxel, *Crusader Nation*, p. 9.
19. Steven J. Diner, *A Very Different Age:*

Americans of the Progressive Era. New York: Hill and Wang, 1998, p. 210.

20. Quoted in Robert S. Gallagher, interview by *American Heritage,* "I Was Arrested, of Course," February 1974. http://americanheritage.com/articles/magazine/ah/1974/2/1974_2_16.shtml.

21. Quoted in McGerr, *A Fierce Discontent,* p. 84.

22. Roger A. Bruns, *Preacher: Billy Sunday and Big-Time American Evangelism.* New York: W.W. Norton, 1992, p. 161.

23. Quoted in Lyle W. Dorsett, *Billy Sunday and the Redemption of Urban America.* Macon, GA: Mercer University Press, 2004, pp. 182–83.

24. Quoted in Ernest Hurst Cherrington, ed., *Anti-Saloon Yearbook 1914.* Westerville, OH: Anti-Saloon League of America, 1914.

25. Theodore Roosevelt, *The Letters of Theodore Roosevelt,* vol. 6, ed. Elting E. Morison et al. Cambridge, MA: Oxford University Press, 1953, p. 1131.

26. Quoted in McGerr, *A Fierce Discontent,* p. 192.

27. McGerr, *A Fierce Discontent,* p. 235.

Chapter Three: Business and Labor Reforms of the Progressive Era

28. McGerr, *A Fierce Discontent,* pp. 15–16.

29. U.S. Bureau of the Census, *Historical Statistics of the United States, Colonial Times to 1970,* Part 1, Series D 11–25, p. 127.

30. McGerr, *A Fierce Discontent,* p. 16.

31. U.S. Bureau of the Census, *Historical Statistics,* Part 1, Series M 271–86, p. 607.

32. U.S. Bureau of the Census, *Historical Statistics,* Part 2, Series Q 389-409, p. 740.

33. Stephen Yafa, *Big Cotton: How a Humble Fiber Created Fortunes, Wrecked Civilizations, and Put America on the Map.* New York: Viking, 2005, p. 84.

34. Quoted in Ray Ginger, *The Bending Cross: A Biography of Eugene Victor Debs.* Piscataway, NJ: Rutgers University Press, 1949, p. 110.

35. Robert H. Zieger and Gilbert J. Gall, *American Workers, American Unions: The Twentieth Century.* Baltimore: Johns Hopkins University Press, 1986, p. 3.

36. John Steele Gordon, *An Empire of Wealth: The Epic History of American Economic Power.* New York: HarperCollins, 2004, p. 250.

37. Quoted in Diner, *A Very Different Age,* p. 67.

38. Jane Addams, "The Settlement as a Factor in the Labor Movement," in *Hull House Maps and Papers* by Residents of Hull House. New York, Crowell, 1895, p. 204.

39. Traxel, *Crusader Nation,* p. 15.

40. Gilder Lehrman Institute of American History, "Progressivism: Anti-Trust," in *The Progressive Era.* www.gilderlehrman.org.

41. McGerr, *A Fierce Discontent,* p. 143.

42. Quoted in John R. Commons et al., *History of Labor in the United States.* New York: Macmillan,1935, pp. 672–73.

43. Quoted in Elliott J. Gorn, *Mother Jones.* New York: Hill and Wang, 2001, p. 216.

Chapter Four: U.S. Presidents of the Progressive Era

44. Quoted in Paul Johnson, *A History of the American People.* New York: HarperPerennial, 1999, p. 617.

45. Quoted in Edmund Morris, *The Rise of Theodore Roosevelt.* New York:

Modern Library, 2001, p. 513.

46. Theodore Roosevelt, "Theodore Roosevelt: First Annual Message, December 3rd, 1901," *The American Presidency Project*, John T. Woolley and Gerhard Peters, University of California at Santa Barbara. www.presidency.ucsb.edu/?pid=29542.

47. Robert L. Reynolds, "The Coal Kings Come to Judgment," *American Heritage,* vol. 11, no. 3, April 1960. www.americanheritage.com.

48. Edith Wharton, *A Backward Glance.* New York: D. Appleton, 1934, p. 311.

49. Morris, *The Rise of Theodore Roosevelt*, p. xxvii.

50. Traxel, *Crusader Nation*, p. 12.

51. Theodore Roosevelt, *An Autobiography.* New York: Macmillan, 1919, p. 302.

52. Theodore Roosevelt, "National Unity Versus Class Cleavage," in *The Writings of Theodore Roosevelt*, ed. William H. Harbaugh. Indianapolis: Bobbs-Merrill, 1967, p. 20.

53. Theodore Roosevelt, "The Man with the Muck-Rake," *Putnam's Monthly and the Critic* 1, October 1906, pp. 42–43.

54. Aida D. Donald, *Lion in the White House: A Life of Theodore Roosevelt.* New York: Basic Books, 2007, p. 193.

55. Woodrow Wilson, *The New Freedom: A Call for Emancipation of the Generous Energies of a People* (1913). Charleston, SC: BiblioBazaar, 2007, p. 14.

Chapter Five: The End of the Progressive Era

56. Walter Lippman, "The World Conflict in Relation to American Democracy," *Annals of the American Academy of Political and Social Science*, vol. 72, 1917, pp. 1–10.

57. McGerr, *A Fierce Discontent*, p. xvi.

58. McGerr, *A Fierce Discontent*, p. 281.

59. Christine M. Kreiser, "The Enemy Within," *American History*, vol. 41, no. 5, December 2006, p. 29.

60. Mark Sullivan, *Our Times: The United States, 1900–1925*, vol 5. New York: Scribner's, 1926–1935, pp. 489–90.

61. Quoted in David Brody, *Labor in Crisis: The Steel Strike of 1919*. Champaign, IL: University of Illinois Press, 1987, p. 146.

62. Quoted in Brody, *Labor in Crisis*, p. 147.

63. Quoted in Brody, *Labor in Crisis*, p. 147.

64. Donald Richberg, *Tents of the Mighty*. Chicago: Willett, Clark, and Colby, 1930, p. 93.

65. John B. Judis, "Are We All Progressives Now?" *American Prospect*, May 8, 2000, p. 36.

66. Ronald Reagan, first inaugural address, January 20, 1981. www.reaganfoundation.org/reagan/speeches/first.asp.

67. Arthur M. Schlesinger Jr., "A Question of Power." *American Prospect*, April 23, 2001, p. 26.

Glossary

anarchist: Someone who rejects all forms of governmental authority as oppressive.

communism: A political system in which the state controls all industry and resources and exerts significant control over its citizenry.

direct democracy: Various legislative provisions that give voters greater authority to influence politics directly; these provisions include reforms such as direct primaries, initiatives, referendums, and recalls.

Eighteenth Amendment: Amendment to the U.S. Constitution ratified in 1919 that prohibited the manufacture and sale of alcoholic beverages.

Gilded Age: Name given to the last two decades of the nineteenth century, when wealthy Americans displayed and spent their fortunes in more flamboyant ways than ever before.

initiative: Political reform measure that gives voters the right to propose laws themselves.

muckrakers: Progressive journalists who use the media, including books and newspaper and magazine stories, to expose political corruption, poverty, exploitation of workers, and other problems in American society.

Nineteenth Amendment: Amendment to the U.S. Constitution ratified in 1920 that gives women citizens the right to vote.

Progressive Era: Period of intense political, economic, and social reform in the United States during the late nineteenth and early twentieth centuries.

Prohibition: Period of U.S. history from 1920–1933 in which the manufacture and sale of almost all alcoholic beverages was outlawed.

radical: An advocate of revolutionary social and political change.

recall: Measure that gives voters the power to remove elected officials from public office.

referendum: Progressive reform measure that gives voters the ability to place laws already approved by legislatures on the ballot so that they can approve or reject them themselves.

robber barons: Negative nickname given to the wealthy industrialists who controlled America's leading corporations in the nineteenth and early twentieth centuries.

Seventeenth Amendment: Amendment to the U.S. Constitution ratified in 1913 that established the direct election of U.S. senators by American voters.

Sixteenth Amendment: Amendment to the U.S. Constitution ratified in 1913 that established a national income tax.

socialism: A social and economic system based on the collective ownership of a state's resources and the total rejection of private ownership of property and resources.

Square Deal: Term used by President Theodore Roosevelt to refer to his promise to bring greater fairness to American business and society.

suffrage: The right to vote.

trust: A powerful combination of firms or companies that can manipulate or control significant aspects of an industry.

For Further Reading

Books

Ann Angel, *America in the 20th Century: 1910–1919*. New York: Marshall Cavendish, 1995. This heavily illustrated resource provides readers with an overview of the United States and its people during the height of the Progressive Era.

Eleanor Clift, *Founding Sisters and the Nineteenth Amendment*. Hoboken, NJ: Wiley, 2003. This book chronicles the struggle for women's suffrage from the mid-1800s all the way to the passage of the Nineteenth Amendment.

John Milton Cooper Jr., *Pivotal Decades: The United States, 1900–1920*. New York: 1990. This comprehensive but readable account of the Progressive Era provides coverage of political and social events and controversies, as well as cultural developments such as motion pictures and radio broadcasting.

Roger Daniels, *American Immigration: A Student Companion*. New York: Oxford University Press, 2001. This work covers the history of immigration to the United States over the years. It includes informative sections on immigration during the Gilded Age and the Progressive Era.

Alex Groner and Editors of *Business Week* and *American Heritage*, *The American Heritage History of American Business and Industry*. New York: American Heritage, 1972. This informative text focuses on the economic, technological, and industrial history of the United States. It includes extensive coverage of American unions, sweatshops, child labor, corporate exploitation of immigrants, and other issues.

Faith Jaycox, *The Progressive Era: An Eyewitness History*. New York: Facts On File, 2005. This book looks at the Progressive Era from a wide range of perspectives, including workers, managers, suffragists, and prohibitionists.

Michael McGerr, *A Fierce Discontent: The Rise and Fall of the Progressive Movement in America*. New York: Oxford University Press, 2005. A fast-paced and informative overview of the Progressive Era and its leading champions.

Milton Meltzer, *Theodore Roosevelt and His America*. London: Franklin Watts, 1994. A biography of famed Progressive Theodore Roosevelt that is especially targeted at young adults.

Web Sites

America 1900 (www.pbs.org/wgbh/amex/1900). This multimedia Web site is a companion to a PBS *American Experience* film of the same name; it focuses on providing a glimpse into "a year in the life of America at the dawn of the 20th century."

How the Other Half Lives, by Jacob Riis (www.yale.edu/amstud/inforev/riis/title.html). This Web site provides the complete text to the famous book by journalist Jacob Riis. This early muckraking work is still regarded as one of the most influential works of literature of the Gilded Age and Progressive Era.

Progressive Era to New Era, 1900–1929 (http://memory.loc.gov/learn/features/timeline/progress/progress.html). A Library of Congress Web site that provides primary sources, photographs, interviews, and other coverage of the first three decades of the twentieth century in America.

Temperance & Prohibition (http://prohibition.osu.edu). A creation of Ohio State University, this Web site provides a wealth of information on the history of temperance and prohibition in the United States.

Theodore Roosevelt: Icon of the American Century (www.npg.si.edu/exh/roosevelt). This Web site is a collaborative effort of the National Portrait Gallery and the Smithsonian Institution. It features a rich assortment of historical information on Roosevelt and his contributions to the Progressive movement.

The Triangle Factory Fire (www.ilr.cornell.edu/trianglefire). A Cornell University Web site that provides exhaustive coverage of the infamous 1911 fire, which came to be a national symbol of corporate exploitation of American workers.

Urban Experience in Chicago: Hull House and Its Neighborhoods, 1889–1963 (www.uic.edu/jaddams/hull/urbanexp). The University of Illinois at Chicago maintains this Web site, which provides multimedia coverage of Jane Addams, Hull House, and the wider issue of urban poverty in America.

Index

Picture Credits

Cover: Library of Congress
AP Images, 9 (upper left), 64, 75
Museé d'Orsay, Paris, France/The Bridgeman Art Library, 8 (upper)
© Bettmann/Corbis, 43, 53, 55, 63, 85
© Underwood & Underwood/Corbis, 60
© Corbis, 11
Gale, Cengage Learning, 29, 74
Hulton Archive/Getty Images, 18, 20, 26, 56, 66, 80, 83, 88
Kean Collection/Getty Images, 25
MPI/Getty Images, 50, 61
Popperfoto/Getty Images, 9 (lower)
Bob Thomas/Popperfoto/Getty Images, 72
Topical Press Agency/Getty Images, 41, 79, 87
Library of Congress, 8 (lower), 9 (upper left), 14, 24, 32, 35, 44, 45, 90
North Wind Picture Archive, 31, 37, 38, 69, 70

About the Author

Kevin Hillstrom has written and edited numerous reference works in the areas of American history and international environmental issues. Credits include *The Cold War—Primary Sourcebook Series* (2006), the nine-volume *Industrial Revolution in America* (2005–2006), the six-volume *World's Environments* (2003–2004), and the four-volume *American Civil War Reference Library* (2000). He has also served as series editor of the *Defining Moments* history reference series.